THE STRAGGLING TOWN

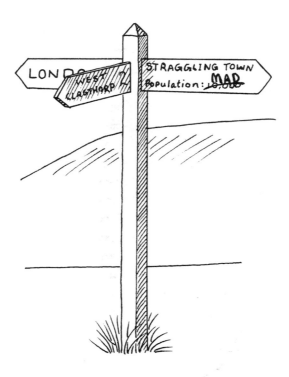

With thanks to Steve Taylor and those at BBC Radio Lancashire who helped to give these stories an airing, and to the late David Parker who first came up with the name 'Straggling Town'.

THE STRAGGLING TOWN:
HILARIOUS TALES OF
LANCASHIRE FOLK

Phil Smith

*with cartoons
by Matt Wilkins*

*To the memory of
Sharon Davie*

Carnegie Publishing Ltd

08435672

First published in 2000 by
Carnegie Publishing Ltd,
Carnegie House,
Chatsworth Road,
Lancaster LA1 4SL

British Library Cataloguing-in-Publication data
A catalogue record for this book is available from the British Library

ISBN 1-85936-079-3

Typeset and originated by Carnegie Publishing Ltd
Printed and bound by Redwood Books, Trowbridge

Contents

Chapter One

Not So New Beginnings

*I*T WAS THE DAWN of the eve of the new millennium in the Straggling Town. A pale sun which had done this sort of thing for rather more millenniums than even Methuselah could count, peeped over the top of Blackedge Moor before throwing a blanket of cloud over his head and going back to bed, as if to say, 'Well, it's a holiday and no one else is getting up, so why should I?'

But the sun was wrong. Down in the Straggling Town quite a few people were up and about. Her-from-Next-Door was already Brassoing the knobs on her pride and joy: the black lead grate that had stood in the back kitchen of her house in Disraeli Street for as many years as the century was old. She never lit it these days, of course, and a dried flower arrangement that she'd done herself out of spikey echinops and other dry and prickly things like her own nature, sat in the hearth. Red Eileen had been up since six taking down the Christmas decorations. She couldn't abide hanging on to useless ornaments, as witness the fact that she'd had three husbands and divorced them all. Her friend Hilda-the-Ton had got up but had gone back to bed with a tray containing three mince pies, a slab of Christmas cake and the remains of the sherry trifle they'd had for tea last night. The tray was now empty and she was unhappily reading an article from *Woman's Own* about a woman who'd had her stomach stapled. Bag o' Nails was lying awake having black thoughts, and Arthur Wormwell was still suffering

abuse from Mrs Wormwell for failing to position the teapot properly under
the spout of the Teasmaid before it went off. Jimmy Capstick was sleeping
fitfully as he had done all night after being persuaded to eat a very
grey-looking pickled egg at the bar of the Poet and Peasant Working Men's
Club the previous night. Only Jurassic Jeff could be said to be sleeping
soundly, but then 12 pints of lager and half-a-dozen Pickup's pies for supper
take quite a bit of sleeping off.

Arthur Hatfield, whose grandfather had clip-clopped in his horse and
cart along the backstreets delivering milk from churns when the century

was only neck height to a milk bottle, buzzed along in
his electric milk float delivering orange juice, Greek
yoghurt and skimmed milk from cows that had never
tasted a blade of Lancashire grass. Times had changed
beyond recognition and the Straggling Town, which
belonged at heart to a world of slopstones, donkeystones,
cobblestones and talk of gallstones huddled round the
fish stall in the open market, was about to be forceps
delivered into a brand new century. Nevertheless, despite
Lancashire's struggles to stay where it was in the cosy,
warm, familiar world of the past, there was a buzz of
excitement brewing, if not over the millennium itself,
over the day and night of celebrations which lay ahead.

After a grand millennium fried breakfast at the Methodist Hall and a walk around the boundaries of the
Straggling Town, there was to be a public bonfire
outside the Poet and Peasant and a grand pie supper.
Fred Pickup and his staff at the pie factory had been
working overtime on the pie and the word 'stupendous',
even though applied by Percy Smallcroft of the local
paper, which had long run out of hyperboles, was
thought not to be out of place on this occasion. Braithwaite's brewery had prepared several barrels of a unique celebratory brew
of such potency that they had decided to call it 'Sleep till February'.

The fried breakfast was a splendid affair containing levels of cholesterol
hitherto only consumed by eskimo whalehunters. For the past 12 months,
Reuben Moorhead had been nourishing a pig called Heathcliffe on milk
and cheese and eggs spiced with the left-overs from the Indian take-away
in Balaclava Street. It had grown so large and spoilt as to have apparently
lost the use of its legs. This was until Fred Chadwick the butcher approached
it with his sticking knife, at which it broke down the sty door and

disappeared with squeals of terror onto the moortop over towards darkest Yorkshire, where everyone assumed it would either pass unnoticed amongst the locals or end up as Barnsley black puddings. But a cunning plan dreamt up at the bar of the Pack o' Lies to lay a trail of cream buns back to the farmhouse soon brought it home. Now Heathcliffe had been reduced to rashers of the most delicious home-cured bacon sizzling in frying pans along with golden free-range eggs, mushrooms, sausages, tomatoes and fried bread to make a Weight Watcher stamp their bathroom scales to pieces for.

By the time we were all replete the sun had had its lie-in and was blinking down somewhat bewilderedly on all the merriment in a town that invented smog and sour-faced mill managers. And we were off to meet it, adults and kids, a motley collection of Straggling Towners, with the notable exception of Bag o' Nails who had failed to turn up to add his own baleful brand of sunshine to the occasion. We climbed out of the shadow of Fiddlers Clough where the night frost still glazed the ferns like icing sugar, and up onto the high moor at Ligginstones where a clever bit of forward planning had paid off. Taking a leaf out of the book of Scott of the Antarctic, the film of which Arthur Wormwell had seen at the Savoy cinema when he was still in short trousers, the day before we'd assembled a survival cairn of Braithwaite's bottled ale, and sarsaparilla for the children, and hidden the whole lot under a pile of bracken. There we fell down upon the springy tufts of nardus grass and for the next half-hour there was the merry hiss of bottle caps being removed and the contented smack of lips as thirsts were slaked. The moorland grouse, known to be firm teetotallers, cackled their disapproval and flew off, practising how to avoid lead shot released from the guns of sozzled country landowners.

The refreshment induced a mood of quiet contemplation as we looked down on the valley that was our home. The sunlight shone like silver on the slate rooftops of the huddled houses.

'A thousand year,' sighed Jimmy Capstick, trying to take in the enormity of time compared to our own littleness. 'What must it have been like a thousand years ago?'

'Wolves!' cried little Gary Parkinson, who had soon got bored with all this sitting about and began running round biting trouser legs and baying loud enough to be heard in Transylvania.

'Vikings and Saxons!' yelled Thomas Greenwood, who'd been listening during history lessons at Corunna Road Junior and Infants Mixed, and he and the rest of the boys took sides and staged a war there in the long grass that would settle the destiny of the Straggling Town for the next thousand years.

By the time we'd beaten the bounds and confirmed every inch of ownership of our unique town, the sun had finished his short winter journey across the sky and was sinking over Widdop reservoir in a pool of crimson light. Someone noticed a puff of steam rising from the chimney of the pie factory.

'Pie's in t' oven!' shouted Arthur Wormwell, and tired legs found new vigour over the last mile down to the Poet and Peasant. Red Eileen, Hilda-the-Ton and a small army of stout and sensible ladies determined to keep alive the arts of home cooking well into the new millennium, had been busy in the kitchen all afternoon. Those parts of Heathcliffe that hadn't found their way into the morning's frying pan had furnished juicy slices of home-baked ham that the ladies were cramming into freshly-made oven-bottom cakes. Sausages, made to Fred Chadwick's prize-winning recipe, were a further tribute to the largesse of Heathcliffe, whose porcine spirit, so full of earthy pleasures, seemed to hover over the proceedings. An equally robust presence in the lard-moutain shape of Jurassic Jeff was busy propping up the bar at the club. Having recently risen from his bed after last night's excesses with a throat like the flue of a Lancashire boiler, Jeff was busy embarking upon another prodigious session of glass-emptying while at the same time casting lustful eyes on the heaving plates of food that were coming out of the kitchen.

But first there was the bonfire. A recent and much-resented addition to the club committee who had put himself in charge of the arrangements was Rowland Slack, son of the reviled Horace Slack, local councillor and money maggot. A great despiser of tradition, he belonged to the new breed of young men at their happiest scattering old ladies from pelican crossings in their four-wheel drives. The passing of the old century would come as no regret to him because he was too busy looking forward to the opportunity the next would bring for him to become fatter, richer and sleeker than his fellow man. And, unable to understand why everyone else didn't see things the same way, he was determined to give the Straggling Town a lesson in being forward-looking and dynamic. He had organised a small ceremony prior to the lighting of the bonfire when various items which represented the old century (and had been extracted from the bosoms of their owners with menaces), were to be thrown onto the bonfire, later to be consumed by the flames of progress and forgotten for ever.

Jonas Metcalf looked on in disbelief as a weft basket full of pyrnes and shuttles and other cherished heirlooms from the old cotton mills, which would have made a tidy bob or two in his junk shop, was thrown onto the wood pile. According to Rowland Slack this would help to rid us of all our silly, sentimental attachment to the old days of the mills. A murmur of dismay came from the older end. Next came the banner from the Mount Zion Methodist Chapel, proudly held aloft on many a Whit Walk before the motorcar and day trips to Camelot sent walking days trudging into the history books. The moths had had a go at the banner and the gold tassles had been chewed by mice, but it still brought a cry of 'Shame!' from Alice Wilkinson who'd once helped to carry it and still kept the bonnet she'd worn that day. Further treasured memories followed until all our yesterdays were piled high on the bonfire waiting to be burnt.

'More moth-eaten memories of the bad old days,' cried Rowland Slack strutting around with fanatical zeal in chilling shades of Nurenberg. 'Ve must look forvard!'

He pointed at the guy that was on top of the bonfire and until now nobody had noticed. In the shadows of the encroaching gloom we could just make out a long bedraggled-looking thing in a flat cap and bracers. 'Who wants to return to that?' shouted the young Slack fervently, switching on his flashlamp to illuminate the full truth of his argument.

And then everyone got a shock. The guy suddenly moved a spindly arm to shade its eyes from the glare.

'Blimey, it's Bag o' Nails!' cried Arthur Wormwell. 'So that's where he's been all day!'

Seated in a battered armchair with a mop in one hand and a bucket in the other was Disraeli Street's answer to Britannia.

'If you're getting rid of the past, you can get rid of me,' boomed Bag o' Nails in his best Old Testament voice. 'Them as destroys our history destroys us.'

'Hear, hear!' we all cried, and there was a burst of applause and a cry of 'Get 'im down, he's a hero'.

Rowland Slack melted off into the darkness red-faced and defeated. And just as we'd rescued the Methodist banner and as many shuttles and other treasures as we could find, Fred Pickup's van arrived with the millennium pie. Two men staggered out with it on a night board and everyone, mesmerised by the wonderful smell, followed them into the club like Bisto kids. There, all thoughts of past and future were forgotten in the all-consuming pleasure of the present. Good food, good ale and good company, What more could you ask for, whatever the century?

Chapter Two

A Burning Issue

*I*T WAS Bag o' Nails' turn to buy fish in the queue on the Open Market. He uncurled a finger like one of those dried foreign sausages and pointed it at a gleaming white enamel tray of haddock fillets.

''Eavy metals,' he pronounced, leadenly. ''Ow do you know that's not full of 'eavy metals?'

He began to deliver a long list of toxic substances, tolling them out with gloomy relish like a funeral bell. In defence of his good name – 'Fleetwood Norman's Always Fresh!' – Fleetwood picked up one of the fillets and flapped it about.

We were being asked to imagine the silvery beast rising through some shimmering spindrift of icy purity. But Bag o' Nails would have none of it. He saw only a leprous thing choking to death in the wake of a North Sea incinerator ship.

'It might look all right, but how do you know what it's like inside?' he argued, and a murmur of collective paranoia arose from the rest of the queue.

Norman whet his boning knife in a dogged attempt at self-control. 'How should I know what's in 'em? What's in the air we breathe? The water we drink? We've got to take these things on trust.'

Far from easing matters, this remark served only to increase the general unrest. To the modern mind the invisible menace of pollution has taken the place of the devil in medieval times.

'We've got more lead water pipes round here than anywhere else in the country,' said Harry Stansfield, who'd been a plumber and knew.

'More waste tips than anyone else,' volunteered Jonas Metcalf, who'd spent a lifetime scavenging the same.

'More nuclear installations,' added Bag o' Nails.

'And look at Khyber Street mill chimley,' cried a voice more corrosive than acid rain. It was Red Eileen who had scented a rumpus like a shark scents blood and had just joined the queue.

Everyone stopped, and eyes were raised towards a long metal cylinder which poked spitefully upwards through the shining wet roof slates. It wasn't a self-respecting old-fashioned chimney, with blackened brickwork and proud stone corbels, belching honest soot that cures blackspot on your roses and triggers off a good cough first thing in the morning to clear out your system. It was some sort of modern alloy thing, so spindly it had to be supported by wires. It was seeping yellow, sickly-looking stuff which hung over the rooftops.

'What is it?' asked a voice.

'I'll tell you what it is,' boomed Bag o' Nails in the voice of a prophet, 'It's death!'

'Come off it,' said Fleetwood, eager to sell some fish before any of it settled.

But Bag o' Nails was not to be put off his mission of doom, he was enjoying it too much. 'They burn things in a furnace there,' he said.

'What sort of things?' demanded Eileen.

'Things nobody else wants,' replied Bag o' Nails darkly.

And there in the Straggling Town market, on a perfectly ordinary Wednesday morning, with Pickup's unloading a fresh batch of pies and the discount record stall playing a rather scratchy rendering of 'What a Wonderful World', Bag o' Nails opened up the dark crypt of his dismal soul. No one there half understood the catalogue of horrors he recited – polychlorinated biphenyls, dioxins, deadly carcinogens – but no one doubted that he knew. Like Doctor Faustus, his studies had been deep, and he wouldn't be content until he'd conjured up the Devil to terrify us all.

'And they're all down there at that factory,' he asserted. And, as if in ghastly confirmation of his words, the smoke suddenly chaged from sickly yellow to bright green, just like the colour of the mushy peas in the Cosy Cafe.

Eileen wanted to march on the factory right away, leading the way with Hilda-the-Ton and Her-from-the-Tripe-Stall. But the idea didn't appeal to Bag o' Nails.

'It's no good,' he said gloomily. 'I've tried writing to the papers. Local radio. Nobody wants to know. Powerful people are behind this. Big money. Bribery and corruption. I've been threatened for trying to open my mouth. They even tried to poison my dog.'

This was too much for Red Eileen who had a soft spot for dogs because unlike husbands they never answered back and knew the meaning of submission. She disappeared in a tremble of indignant henna to round up her troops.

Ten minutes later, Eileen and her war-party arrived in Khyber Street, just as a silver chauffeur-driven Rolls-Royce was gliding towards the factory gates. Without any hesitation Eileen stepped out into the road. A stint as a lollipop lady had given her a distinct air of authority over moving vehicles, and the chauffeur brought the car to an abrupt standstill. A window slid noiselessly open like the curtains at a crematorium.

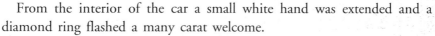

'All right, what's going on?' she demanded. She really should have said, 'What's going up?' because at that moment the smoke from the chimney changed from bright green to red.

A voice was heard from the rear of the limousine. It came from deep within the cream leather upholstery, as if a soft fat wallet had spoken. The chauffeur promptly got out and opened the back door.

'Ladies,' he announced, 'Mr Leech would like you to join him.'

From the interior of the car a small white hand was extended and a diamond ring flashed a many carat welcome.

Eileen was disarmed. Her pin jammed. She had never been faced with charm before. Huge Hilda and Her-from-the-Tripe-Stall melted like so much marshmallow.

The three women piled into the back of the Rolls-Royce and it purred off into the factory. The rest of us finally caught up with them several hours later back in the market at the Cosy Cafe. I've never seen Eileen drunk before and I don't want to again. The uncompromising scourge of malekind had collapsed into a milk pudding of sentiment.

'What a luverly man,' she sighed, her eyes glazed as cocktail cherries.

'Yes,' oozed Hilda, all saggy like warm dough.

'What did he say about the toxic waste?' demanded Bag o' Nails.

''Sperfectly safe,' said Eileen.

'We've been invited to a party at his house,' simpered Hilda.

'He's got a swimming pool,' sighed Her-from-the-Tripe-Stall dreamily.

'And a minstrel's gallery,' added Hilda.

'He's luverly,' repeated Eileen with a look in her eyes that rated an X certificate. 'He's our friend.'

'Jezebels!' roared Bag o' Nails. 'You've been bought.'

But suddenly, the three sisters of the Cosy Cafe recovered their ferocity and fell upon him and began removing the skin from his bones.

It was a bad case, I suppose, of the messenger being shot for bringing the bad news in the first place. Many people said it served Bag o' Nails right for being such a misery. And he probably enjoyed it.

Chapter Three

Of Pies and Men

*B*Y HALF-PAST NINE every morning in the Straggling Town there's always a fair queue at the pie stall. It's the time when the day's first batch arrives straight from Fred Pickup's bakery. Catch a Pickup's pie now, and it's just at its best: not too hot to cause any injuries, but warm enough for the juice to run when you sink your teeth into one. But still the Devil of a job to transport without rupturing the fragile pastry case and losing the sublime juices to the pavement or the fluffy corners of a shopping bag. So that's why, to the happy clarion call of 'Pies are 'ere,' people would rush for the stall and often consume them there and then, like starving street urchins. Childhood injunctions never to be seen eating in the street were always ignored in the case of a Pickup's pie. The more scrupulous might be seen guzzling theirs at the back of the greengrocery stall, amongst the orange boxes and cabbage trimmings so as not to be thought of as common. Many a fur coat and pin-striped suit has been seen to emerge with fresh gravy stains down their fronts, along with a great to-do of smacking of lips to try and rid them of that wonderful stickiness conferred by proper gelatine made from boiled pig's trotters and not nastiness from a boneyard.

As usual, Jurassic Jeff was the first in the queue. No one dare usurp his place. Jurassic sported a belly like a full beer-barrel, tattoos of such striking beligerence (daggers dripping with blood and headless corpses and things) that everywhere he went was immediately declared a war zone and the BBC sent Kate Adie, and a head as hairless as a bullet set upon a neck that was a plinth of lard and the envy of the whole of Padiham for thickness. But don't be deceived by appearances. He may have looked uncouth but Jeff had the most refined taste buds outside the kitchens of the Café Royal. And this, despite stunning them every night with a gallon or more of ice-cold, chemically-treated lager. He was the best judge of a meat pie since Desperate Dan. And this was all down to experience.

Following the local football team through thick and thin had made Jeff a connoisseur of pies and pasties up and down the land. He could remember every pie he'd ever consumed. Gristly at Grimsby. Magic at Mansfield. Diarrhoea at Doncaster. Jeff recalled them all as well as he did the result, the scorers, who was sent off and how to find every public house within throwing-up distance of the ground. He was a walking pie and football Wisden.

And, just in case there's any of those posh gastronomers around poo-pooing this accomplishment, let me ask them, could they recognise a Brentford-beef-and-onion smuggled into a batch of Torquay torpedoes while blindfolded and under the influence of a gallon and a half of Carling Black Label? Such things are not to be sniffed at – especially some of the football pies.

Jurassic Jeff lost no time in sinking his teeth – the only part of his body not tattooed – into the first of the six pies he'd purchased. He tackled it

a bit like an Ascot toff might set about a Whitstable oyster, the lid well up to his chin to avoid spilling any of the delectable juice. But there followed a noise you would not be likely to hear from a well-bred picnic party seated around a Rolls-Royce. It was a slurping sound like a shingle beach being dredged and then such a slapping of the lips you'd have thought you were in a zoo full of sealions clapping for their supper.

Taking a breather before starting the next pie, Jeff looked up and spotted us. Clutching the bag containing the rest of the pies with all the delicacy of a rhino carrying a nest of birds' eggs, he barrelled towards us.

'Hey up!' he cried. Jurassic's mouth was mightier than an aerial bombardment from an Iraqui supergun, and he launched into a murderous tirade against the referee at Saturday's football match.

'Pies all right?' asked Arthur Wormwell, doing his best to divert the conversation to something less inflamatory. Jurassic's temperament was like the earthquake zone in the earth's crust, you never knew when the next eruption would take place.

Jeff didn't need to answer. He sucked at the contents of the next pie like a thirsty camel and was overcome by what I can only describe as rapture. He was transformed from a raging bull into a cherub. A warm flush enveloped the tattooed daggers on his neck and his skin-head shone like a halo. I could have sworn I saw a tear shining in the corner of his eye, though to suggest as much to Jeff would have been inviting a broken nose. He floated away like a bit off the ceiling of the Sistine Chapel.

'Holy Moses,' cried Arthur as we watched him go. 'Think of the potential of Pickup's pies on the criminally prone. A free supply once a day and our prisons would soon be empty. I think I'll write to the Home Secretary.' But not everyone appreciated the transformation.

'Just look at it,' came a voice like battery acid, once Jeff was safely out of earshot. Red Eileen and the ponderous Hilda-the-Ton had put in an appearance on the market.

'Fat and pasty, all beer and pies.'

'You are what you eat,' chimed-in Hilda, who must have been eating nothing but whale meat since the War. And where did that put Eileen? We didn't have long to wait for an answer. She ordered roll-mop herrings from the fish stall, all bitter and twisted.

'And a pound o' cod.' She said. She cast a cold and watery eye in our direction. 'You chaps want to watch the company you keep,' she warned darkly.

'Oh, you don't want to judge him by the outside,' responded Arthur. 'The proof of the pie ...'

'Pudding,' interrupted Eileen sourly. 'It's the proof of the pudding.'

'Pudding, pie, what's the difference?' said Arthur, wilting a bit.

'There's a lot of difference,' shouted Hilda. 'If my husband asks for a steak pudding and I bring him a pie, there's bother.'

We found it difficult to imagine that Hilda's husband ever caused her any bother. It would be a bit like the wake from a dinghy threatening an oil-tanker.

Eileen curled her lip in such a sneer you could make out the real colour of her lips under her livid lipstick. They were blue, like lips can go after eating too much vinegar.

'Young people don't know what they're eating these days. They'll eat owt. Any old rubbish. And that's why this generation's such a load of rubbish,' she concluded with a final burst of venom.

Just then an Atlantic depression blew in. Bag o' Nails. Today he looked even more cadaverous than usual. A sick corpse, if you can have such a thing.

'Not so good today?' I ventured.

Bag o' Nails held his stomach. 'Something I ate,' he growled morosely.

That was it, we thought. If you are what you eat, Bag o' Nails is food poisoning.

His eyes settled on the pie stall. 'I had one of their pies for me tea.'

He looked round dolefully. 'That's the trouble these days. You never know what you're eating.'

Here we go again, we thought. The world of Hieronymus Bosch descends upon the Straggling Town. The medieval imagination running riot among the pikelets and pickled cabbage. Fleetwood Norman picked up his boning knife ready to defend his fish from the usual assault from heavy metals and hideously deforming radioactive isotopes.

'Now, look here,' he wagged. 'If you think you've come to start your usual scaremongering ...'

'Fishmonger Attacks Scaremonger' thought Percy Smallcroft from the local paper, who always thinks in headlines.

But at that moment, sensing trouble like a Great White senses blood, Jurassic Jeff reappeared. But the pies had truly worked their miracle. He stood in front of Bag o' Nails, and instead of Godzilla meets Dr Death, it was a perfectly amicable encounter.

'Fancy a pie?' said Jeff, proffering the bag.

No one refuses Jurassic Jeff.

'Er, thanks a lot,' faltered Bag o' Nails and bit gingerly into the shell.

'Be careful,' warned Jeff, and fear danced into Bag o' Nails' eyes.

'Don't want to spill the juice do we? Best bit.'

Chapter Four

Watch This Space!

*T*HERE IS SOMETHING ELSE besides our pies, ready wit and general amiability for which the Straggling Town is justly renowned. And that is the number of times we appear to be visited by creatures from Outer Space. Perhaps, having heard about all these other things, our celestial neighbours have put us on some galactic package tour, but so far no little green men or frightful creatures dripping corrosive acid from their extendable jaws have been spotted queuing for Pickup's pies on the Market. Though Jurassic Jeff's tattoos, conceived by a Blackpool tattoo artist spaced out on another sort of acid, have a similar nightmarish quality. But whoever they may be, having journeyed across countless light-years to get here, they have never thought it worth their while to stop, until now. This year alone, reported cases of unexplained lights in the sky have equalled the large number of licensed premises in the town – a connection some of us have not failed to observe. Others point to the frequency of high-powered torches being used at dead of night on the surrounding moortops as sheep are rounded up into unmarked vehicles by men in balaclavas. Others, of an equally rational turn of mind like to remind us of the fact that we are on the flight path into Manchester airport. But most of us want nothing to do with these mundane explanations. We passionately want to believe that there is something going on out there, if for no other reason than that there's not a lot going on down here. Disappointed minds unoccupied by work and money, on account of the fact that there's not much of either to be had in the Straggling Town, are only too happy to reach to the stars for some excitement. Each day we post someone on the main road into the town in the hope that they will report the imminent arrival of agents Mulder and Scully.

If alien eyes had happened to be watching through the broken cloud over the Market this morning, they'd have witnessed a typical scene. There was the wet fish queue, kinked as usual to avoid the opprobrium of standing too close to the saucy second-hand bookstall, and inching as close as possible to the pie stall where a fresh batch of Pickup's pies was doing unearthly things to human nostrils. Eileen was busy forging her way to the front of the queue with the help of a shopping bag weighted with ten pounds of Ormskirks and a pair of steel knitting needles poking viciously through the sides. In her red mac and wellingtons, with the striking bouffant of henna-dyed hair piled like a beacon fire on top of her head, she would have been clearly visible to any casual observer from Alpha Centuri. So would her friend Hilda-the-Ton, on account of the extraordinarily large surface area of the globe that her mountainous girth takes up. Bag o' Nails, our own megalith of misery, would definitely have remained invisible because of the dark cloud of pessimism which permanently hangs over him.

Fleetwood Norman's boning knife was flashing busily as he unzipped the innards of a pair of herrings, and Eileen was doing a similar job on the character of the senior reporter of the *Straggling Town Examiner*, Percy Smallcroft.

'He's off his trolley,' she cried with such a frightful snap of her dentures that we thought a live shark had surfaced from the depths of Fleetwood Norman's mobile fish van.

She brandished the front page of the latest edition of the paper. In headlines likewise large enough to be visible from deep space were the words:

'LOOK OUT! THEY ARE HERE!'

The story was that the odious hack, returning across the moors late one night from a drinking session at the Sniggering Sheep, had experienced an encounter of such a close kind that a full two hours of his miserable life had mysteriously elapsed. Now it's not unusual for periods of time to disappear unaccounted for after drinking sessions at the Sniggering Sheep. But we were being asked to believe that in Percy's case, he had been carried aboard an alien craft and experimented upon by what he described as 'shimmering angels', several shaky drawings of which were included as evidence of his abduction.

Now anyone at all familiar with Percy Smallcroft's habits could understand medical science's interest in him, alien or human.

How a liver, pickled like a gherkin by alcohol for so many years could continue to function was indeed a miracle. For students of the moral sciences of mankind he could prove just as interesting. A journalistic career, supposed to be based on the pursuit of truth, which had been devoted to nothing but lies, gossip, slander and false innuendo, would make a fascinating study. But alien interest in such a form of low-life? Surely this was too far-fetched even for the stoutest believers in extra-terrestrials.

Red Eileen, whose down-to-earth views on human nature were based on the close and contemptuous observations of no fewer than three husbands, all of whom had convinced her that the twin pivots of male motivation were drink and 'a bit on the side', continued to scoff until her lividly painted lips curled like a bloodied sickle.

'Shimmering angels, our slopstone,' she sneered. 'Sounds like that trollop from the General Hospital. And there's only one 'experiment' she knows.'

The newspaper was passed eagerly around for us to study Percy's sketches of his abductors. They bore a remarkable resemblance to the flouders to be found on Fleetwood Norman's fish slab. In fact they even seemed to glow like those caught off the Cumbrian coastline despite passionate denials from British Nuclear Fuels and, of course, Fleetwood himself.

'I don't know why they didn't take him away for good, like so much moon rock, the lunatic,' growled the fishmonger, sensing a conspiracy against his fish.

'It proves they're compassionate individuals,' suggested Arthur, buoyed by a vision of a caring socialist universe beyond the dog-eat-dog of earthly market forces.

'Any creature of compassion would have done us all a favour and got rid of him forever,' snarled Eileen.

But, like old soldiers, raddled hacks never die, they just fade away like printer's ink, and at that moment the man himself made an appearance. Several of us crowded round him, but not Bag o' Nails who was convinced he would still be radioactive. The repulsive little pip-squeak had never enjoyed such celebrity and began to swell visibly like roasting popcorn. His round, fat face looked remarkably red, giving some credence to Bag o' Nails' theory of radioactive exposure. But Arthur insisted it was the hack's normal beer-flush.

'What I want to know is, why did they choose you?' boomed Bag o' Nails.

Percy swelled to near bursting point. 'Probably,' he puffed, 'because of my unique position as a journalist, close to the hearts and minds of the people of this town.'

A very large and violent raspberry emerged from a pair of very scarlet lips. But Percy ignored it, raising a copy of his newspaper.

'But there's more to come,' he cried. 'So watch this space!' And with a marked degree of gravitational wobble, he veered off towards the bridge of the Pack o' Lies pub to steer down a few more lunchtime pints.

Most sensible observers concluded that the whole episode was only a publicity stunt to boost the circulation figures of the paper. Nevertheless it didn't stop us catching up with our own stars in the paper's weekly horoscope, nor studying the Births, Marriages and Deaths columns for the true meaning of human life. But then we do that every week without alien intervention.

Chapter Five

Holy Rupture

*T*HE WIND HOWLED through the open market like a swarm of demons. It rattled the awnings and sent clouds of litter swirling into the air like demented seagulls. People huddled together, which was nothing new in a town which invented gossip. And, of course, we grumbled, something else we're good at.

But then another noise rose above the wind. It sounded like clogs being dragged across a cattlegrid. It was the hectic strumming of a guitar, amplified to distraction. And, wafting over the stalls of pale tripe and faded denim, came the words:

'God's a good guy, so reach for the sky!
Heaven's above, feel Jesus' lurve.'

The evangelists had come to save the world and, like a child who tackles his peas before the chicken nuggets, had decided to take on the worst bits first, starting with our town.

Red Eileen arrived like a Viking longship, her red bouffant defying both wind and gravity. 'What's all this, then?' she demanded in a tone that would have sent St Paul packing.

'We're going to be saved!' cried Her-from-Next-Door, with a wicked challenging glint in her small eye. The only kind of saving she understood was 5p off a packet of cream crackers at Kwik Save.

Now I don't want to give the impression that we're a Godless lot in the Straggling Town. It's just that all this raw, soul-baring, evangelical stuff is foreign to our natures. We're more likely to be closet Christians who keep God locked away for Sundays with Thora Hird on the box and the occasional visit to church when the grand-children are baptised. God's too big for us to be on first name terms with and too baffling, destroying dinosaurs and steering galaxies into infinity. We're polite to vicars because we've been brought up that way, and who'd live in that draughty old vicarage with smokeless at £8 a bag? Even Eileen's on her best behaviour

with vicars. She wouldn't hesitate to get out her best china and open a
Battenburg cake if one called, even though she's never set foot in church
since her first marriage, before her hair turned red and when mistaken men
thought she looked demure.

They'd stopped singing now and had started to mingle with the crowd
on the market, doing their converting. You could see folk stiffen, like you
do when you see a Jehovah's Witness coming down the backyard.

'They'd better not try owt wi' me,' muttered Bag o' Nails.

He was right. I felt like warning them. In his heyday, before cynicism
completely warped his planks, Bag o' Nails had founded a humanist society
which met every Tuesday night in the Co-op Rooms. He'd once picketed
Corunna Road school to try to get them to stop prayers in assembly.

A man with the flea-bitten look of a middle-aged mole-catcher approached. 'Jesus saves,' he began.

'Aye, with the Bradford and Bingley, I suppose,' grunted Bag o' Nails,
straight onto the offensive.

The evangelist didn't look a bit religious. If the eyes are supposed to be
the windows of the soul, his needed cleaning. He looked distinctly shifty.
No long, searching glances that pierced you to the quick. No blazing gaze
to flush out your cowering soul from its shadows. He looked more like a
man fast running out of time, an overworked porter with one eye on the
engine-driver trying to bundle you onto a train and get the door shut. But
then I don't suppose they can all look like those pictures of Jesus we used
to have at Sunday school in a white nightie with arms outstretched and
eyes that would melt the heart of a wheel-clamper.

He ignored Bag o' Nails and turned to Arthur. 'Brother, why not join
us?' said the evangelist, pushing a leaflet into his hand like a celestial
time-share salesman.

But Bag o' Nails wasn't going to be kept out of this. As a man who
had spent a lifetime moaning about everything under the sun, he wasn't
going to be denied a direct line to the real perpetrator of human misery.
He poked the evangelist in the back with one of his giant sausage-like
fingers, right between where wings might be expected to sprout.

'Suffering,' he bellowed. 'Ow do you account for 'uman suffering?'

The mole-catcher's eyes darted wildly, looking for an escape route. The
whistle had gone. The train was leaving. Here was one who was definitely
being left behind.

'Er,' he stammered, searching the tripe stall for inspiration. But only
piles of pale crumpets confronted him, full of holes like bad arguments.

'Well?' demanded Bag o' Nails, with ferret-like remorselessness. His eyes glowed like coals. His missus had spent two years in agony dying of cancer, as meek and harmless a creature as ever drew breath.

'Who are we to comprehend God's will?' ventured the evangelist.

'Pooh!' exploded Bag o' Nails, rattling the awning over the tripe stall. 'I'll tell you what it is. It's because God's not there. And niver has bin!' He swept his huge arms in a gesture of triumphant despair. 'We're a haccident! A bloody cosmic haccident! That's what we are!'

This brand of extremism was too much for Red Eileen. It was all right not to bother too much about religion, everyone did it. But to go around denouncing it. Well, that wasn't respectable. That was striking a blow at everything this country stood for: God Save The Queen and the Church of England.

'Hey, you. Watch your language!' she said, making her lips so tight and small they almost disappeared, showing only a razor-thin scar of livid lipstick.

'Move along there, will you?' shouted Fleetwood Norman from the back of his fish van. He was getting rather fed up of religion getting in the way of the smooth progress of capitalism. The fisher-of-men saw his opportunity and fled from this hotbed of scepticism. Reason wasn't part of his repertoire. Evangelism feeds off hungry hearts not bitter intellects like Bag o' Nails's.

But the interlude had left us unsettled. 'They're burying Puffing Billy today,' said Bag o' Nails gloomily.

Billy had defied death as stoutly as anyone. Sixty Capstan full-strength a day over half-a-century, he'd keeled over at the bar of the Cock and Bottle reaching for his lighter. The air in the town was already noticeably sweeter. But he'd be missed. Somehow he'd been a touchstone for all our excesses. If Billy could cheat the Reaper, we all stood a chance. There'd be a crowd outside the library as there always was on such occasions, waiting for the hearse to go past.

We decided to join them. All this talk of religion had depressed us. We needed a good funeral to cheer us up.

There was a good turn out despite the wind. Drips hung glistening on noses. Red capillaries twisted under blue cheeks. There was a lot of shuffling and coughing and people spoke in whispers. Even the cider drinkers had broken camp out of respect for this solemn gathering of the Straggling Town elders. Finally, the hearse slid past and the caps were removed. White and naked heads defying the wind.

'Where's he going, then?' demanded Bag o' Nails, bitter to the last.

'Cemetery,' replied a voice. 'Didn't fancy the crematorium.'

'Surprising for such a heavy smoker.'

'No,' persisted Bag o' Nails. 'I mean after that.'

We shifted uneasily. No one spoke. In the distance you could hear the evangelists strike up again with remorseless cheerfulness. It was 'Christians Awake!', again.

'Huh,' grunted Bag o' Nails, and, aiming his giant chin into the teeth of the wind, he set off home.

Chapter Six

A Tale of Talents

*W*ITH AN ALMIGHTY RUMBLE the chapel wall hit the ground, sending a cloud of dust into the sky which hung there, doing its best to hide the shameful scene from the eyes of God. The Mount Zion Methodist Chapel, AD 1873, had tumbled like the walls of Jerico.

'Tertius Butterworth will be turning in his grave,' observed an onlooker, shepherded to a respectful distance by a policeman, well out of the way of any flying hymn books.

But the chapel's founder no longer had a grave to turn in. Weeks earlier the graveyard had been cleared and the mortal remains of the pious exhumed under cover of darkness by a team of workmen encouraged by a handsome bonus to complete the grisly task in double quick time.

Jonas Metcalf hurried past with a cart full of mildewed hassocks which he had plans to resurrect as footstools. The stained glass and oak panelling had already gone to refurbish the Mad Hatters pub down the road, and the pulpit had been shipped out to America where it would find its way into the boardroom of a large corporation renting-out one-armed bandits.

But the real money would be made out of the stone which was now disappearing onto the back of one of Fred Higson's lorries. This would be resold at a breathtaking profit for use in tasteful new executive homes, with the extra-special recommendation that the houses so constructed would be forever free of domestic strife on account of the stone being impregnated with the prayers of the righteous. Handling such stones had already brought Fred closer to Heaven than most. For he was rich enough to own a light aircraft which he flew every Sunday from Squires Gate airport.

By the time the dust had settled, the only thing left to indicate that a place of worship had stood there for over a century was a noticeboard which proclaimed:

'Enter into the joy of the Lord.' Matthew 25.

Arthur Wormwell, D-I-Y scholar and dangerous left-wing thinker, sniffed sceptically.

'Only if you're a stinking capitalist,' he said.

Fred Chadwick, the butcher, who was on his way to the bank to stow away a particularly satisfying morning's takings and had just stopped like everyone else to watch the end of an era, took this to be some kind of remark intended for him and removed a large blood-stained fist from his coat-pocket. It hastened an explanation from Arthur.

'Matthew 25. The parable of the talents: "Unto him who hath shall be given, and him that hath not shall be taken away even that which he hath". It's a capitalist's charter,' said Arthur. 'Double your money and you're OK, you go to heaven. Fail to make it grow and it's Outer Darkness. Weeping and gnashing of teeth.'

'Quite right,' said a woman with a dead fox pinned to her back who was just off to the bank with her divi from her water shares.

'There's never been such a talented age,' went on Arthur, warming to his subject like a lay preacher on Ecstasy. 'People can make money out of anything these days. You can't move for corporate accountants in two-tone shirts oozing Eau de Cologne, dreaming up ways of making us pay for what used to be free. It was once called Beveridge. Now it's called pilferage. From the cradle to the grave, pay, pay, pay. They're working on a meter to fasten on your nose to measure how much fresh air you breathe so that they can start to charge you.'

'They're not?' cried a gullible woman who'd once gone to the Co-op to ask for a free Nelson Mandela because she'd seen it written on a fly poster.

Arthur ignored her as he continued his Pentecostal tirade. 'These days they even charge you to park at the hospital. If you forget to pay when your heart-attack flares up again, you'll be wheel-clamped, with a fixed charge big enough to put you straight back into intensive care. That's why they're pulling all the churches down,' concluded Arthur, waving his arms around like a deranged moth-catcher. 'There's no need of 'em. The Lord is well-pleased with his good and faithful capitalist servants. The rest can go and –'

'Weep and gnash?' I suggested, as the inspiration began to flag. The mention of hospitals had brought a sudden animation to Arthur's ageing audience, like a shot of adrenalin straight to the heart. Apart from a good road traffic accident, mugging or murder, nothing is more guaranteed to get old people excited than the subject of hospitals. At the slightest mention of the surgical removal of diseased organs, the chronic sick will take up their beds and walk. The dead in the Straggling Town have even been known to return to life to discuss the details of what carried them off.

Vaguely aware that what was going on probably constituted an unlawful gathering – gall-bladders and things were suddenly being discussed – the policeman moved us on. But the spark of revolution lit by Arthur had preceeded us onto the Market, because by the time we arrived there was a fair conflagration going. Not, let it be said, fuelled by any widespread concern for the fate of life's poor weepers and gnashers, but by what was seen by the honest stall-holders as an even more fundamental threat – to their pockets. A plan to introduce double-yellow lines onto the streets round the market and force motorists onto the town's pay-and-display car parks had provoked universal fury. As we arrived at the wet-fish stall Fleetwood Norman was demonstrating on a fillet of coley what he would like to do with the town's chief executive officer.

'Cut 'em off!' cried Eileen, who may have been referring to what she wanted doing with the heads on her half-pound of sprats, though a glance at her face told otherwise. Her-from-the-Tripe-Stall opposite took up her sister's cry and began doing things with a tray of chitterlings which had our eyes watering.

'They'll go to the supermarkets where there's free parking,' moaned Fleetwood. 'They're bleeding this town dry.'

'Wait till they build another supermarket now they've pulled down the chapel,' said Arthur, dowsing the flames with petrol.

The uproar was drowned by a sudden explosion of sound. It was as if the Boys' Brigade bass drummer had taken up position in the pit of everyone's stomach and started to pound away.

It was the new breed of market trader summoning his customers to come and buy his cut-price jeans. A clarion call to youth, of amplified pop music to turn us all deaf as cobbles.

'Lord!' cried Arthur, and we left while our eardrums were still intact.

As we walked home the sight of the huge gap left by the demolished chapel brought on a heavy bout of soul-searching.

'Why have I never been any good at making money?' moaned Arthur.

'I suppose,' I ventured, 'because when we were at school nobody seemed to mention it. Like sex. Nobody took you to one side and said, "Get as much as you can, lad. Get a big car and a fancy house, and beggar the rest of 'em. That's what it's all about". Instead, it was endless lectures about doing good and being a useful member of society.'

'And not wearing drainpipe trousers,' added Arthur.

'What will become of us?' I asked.

'Weeping and gnashing of teeth,' said Arthur. And then, 'We'll be lucky if we can afford any teeth. There'll be no National Health Service.'

'Weeping and gnashing of gums?' I suggested, and we trudged on towards the Outer Darkness.

Chapter Seven

Sitting in Judgment

THE COVEN was busily at work in the cafe in the Market. There was Red Eileen, Hilda-the-Ton and Her-from-Next Door. They were crouched round the red formica topped table like crones round a clay effigy. The air was heavy with malice. Someone was in for it.

'Stark naked she was,' said Her-from-Next-Door, kneading her words with her lips to squeeze out every ounce of juiciness. Hilda-the-Ton, who filled the corner of the tiny cafe with her tremendous bulk, stared aghast from the plinth of her many chins.

'All over?'

'Every inch,' averred Her-from-Next-Door, sticking to her story despite the wilting stare of the Red One.

'And in Gladstone Park!' gasped Hilda.

'Behind the rhododendrons, right next to the pitch-and-put where some teenage boys from St Paul's were playing.'

'She was asking for it,' hissed Eileen, her eyes narrowing as if she was deciding just where to place the pin to inflict most damage.

'She got it,' announced Her-from-Next-Door triumphantly, and the others leant forward to savour the kill.

Unfortunately, that was all we managed to hear, as at that moment two plates full of steak-pudding, chips and bright green mushy peas steamed their way onto the table in front of us along with a very garrulous Doris from behind the counter. It put paid to our earwigging just as effectively as sudden deafness.

On the open market the wind was funnelling across the car park, discouraging any topless sunbathing on the seats outside the Job Centre. The topic of conversation being skinned and boned in the wet fish queue was vandalism. Fleetwood Norman's fish van had itself become an overnight victim. The illustration on the side showing a line of smiling fish swimming happily into an open net, along with the celebrated caption, 'Fleetwood Norman's Always Fresh', had been cruelly defaced. Spectacles and moustaches, and other appendages not fit to be mentioned, had been added to the fish along with a new slogan: 'Fish do it without touching.'

As we arrived, various remedies to rid our nation of this cancer were being offered, the most humane of which involved cutting off the culprits' hands. So inflamed had become some of the older members of the queue that we began to fear for the safety of two young men browsing at the record stall oblivious to the danger. They belonged to that exotic genus of youth which most closely resembles a cockatoo caught in an oil-slick. Their heads were shaven apart from a greased and multi-coloured plume. Every time they moved there was a dull clank of assorted ironmongery which had been impaled to various parts of their person.

The trouble with punks, even in the Straggling Town, normally very tolerant of eccentricities, is that they can so easily be seen as a symbol for all that is wrong with the world, particularly amongst the elderly. It's not at all clear how lads who spend the best part of their lives in their bedrooms drinking instant coffee and listening to heavy metal music, or stuck in front of the bathroom mirror trying to get their hair to stand on end or a safety-pin through their noses, could be to blame for the abuse of power and pursuit of corporate self-interest which is at the root of most human misery. But as far as Harry Cartwright was concerned that's just what they were.

Ironically, Harry, a leading light of the British Legion bore distinct resemblances to the punks. He had his own chain – a fob, draped across his waistcoat. Where hair still grew, his head had been scalped just as assiduously. And though he didn't have a plume, a fair old quantity of kitchen soap had gone into training the spikes of his sergeant-major moustache so that they stuck out nearly as far as his ears. And although he'd rather have died than wear a t-shirt with a picture of the German

Imperial eagle on it, he did have a blazer with the regimental badge of the Old Contemptibles.

'Give up, Harry,' pleaded Mrs Cartwright at his side, white curls under a grey plastic rain hood. But Harry was back in the Western Desert. He marched towards the punks, collecting a rather bloody dishcloth from Fleetwood Norman's counter on the way. He thrust the cloth into the hands of the nearest youth.

'Clean it!' roared the old soldier, the tips of his moustache quivering like poisonous darts.

'Clean what, dad?' asked the lad amiably.

The suggestion of any filial connection between this treacherous parakeet and himself brought on a near apoplexy in Harry. His face took on the colour of the plastic ketchup tomatoes in the market cafe.

'Come away, Harry. Come away,' implored his wife. But Harry had faced Rommel and his tanks. He had bayonetted a retreating Italian in the buttocks. He wasn't going to back off from a kid with earrings.

His stick was raised when a yell like a works' hooter interrupted things.

'Jason! What's going on?'

Red Eileen had arrived with her own artillery in tow in the shape of a Sherman tank named Hilda.

Jason looked abashed. His plume toppled.

'Get home, this minute,' cried the shrill one. 'And turn the oven on.'

Whether Jason was expected to put his head in the oven or it was for reheating the meat and potato pies she was brandishing wasn't clear. The issue paled into insignificance beside the amazing revelation that Eileen, the most terrifying disciplinarian on the planet, had a son who was a punk.

Eileen sorted things out in the time it takes the arrival of the Black Maria to quell a weekend fracas outside the chip shop. Her son couldn't have had anything to do with the graffiti, she said. He'd been at home all night washing his hair. And, in any case, if he'd have even thought about it he'd have been dead before he could do it.

The incident had taken our minds off the Gladstone Park business, but it wasn't long before we learnt of the outcome.

Arthur called next morning to see if I would go with him to the magistrates court. (Yes, we do have a local magistrates court. Not everything in the Straggling Town is resolved by casting runes round a table in the Cosy Cafe.) It was Rodney from next door, Arthur explained. He was in trouble.

Rodney is a bit backward. What they used to call 'ten pence t' t'bob', an expression that doesn't translate too well into the new currency. He was a big, overgrown lad but with a child's brain. He couldn't work and spent most of his time out by the side of the main road waving to the passing traffic. Everyone who passed pipped and this pleased him no end and made him feel important and loved.

The court was full. We all had to stand up when the magistrates filed in. The senior magistrate looked familiar.

'Isn't that what's-his-name …?' I whispered to Arthur, searching my memory.

The case against Rodney was heard. He was charged with indecently exposing himself to a young lady who had been minding her own business sun-bathing in the park.

Rodney's mother spoke in her son's defence. He was an innocent. The worst he'd done was go for a wee in the bushes. Whereas the young lady in question was no better than she should have been. She wasn't wearing any clothes. This was against the park by-laws. She'd checked at the town hall.

'Two wrongs don't make a right,' said the magistrate gravely, drawing on the deepest reserves of his magisterial training. 'Let the boy speak for himself.'

This was ridiculous and everyone indicated as much. Nevertheless, Rodney was ushered to his feet. He wore a broad grin and waved happily at everyone as if they were passing motorists.

'Aay, bless him,' cried Her-from-Next-Door, who was at the front with Eileen and Hilda. The clerk scowled at her and would have said something but thought better of it when he saw Eileen's face.

'Well?' demanded the magistrate impatiently, glancing at his watch and thinking of his smoked salmon lunch with the Rotary. 'What were you doing in the rhododendron bushes?'

Then I suddenly remembered who the magistrate was. It was Adrian Fullshaw, leading light in the parish church youth club, 1958. We all went on a trip to Blackpool illuminations and he got drunk; mooning down the Golden Mile from the back window of a Laycock's luxury coach. We were stopped by the police and he got fined.

'It's ...' I whispered to Arthur. He nodded.

'In view of the extreme gravity of the offence, I have no alternative ...' said the magistrate.

Then Arthur rose to his feet and cleared his throat. He looked straight at Adrian Fullshaw.

'Let him who is without guilt cast the first stone,' he said.

The magistrate recognised us instantly. He turned white, coughed, turned briefly to his colleagues on the bench and announced, 'Case dismissed.'

Everyone clapped. Rodney grinned even more. The clerk to the court moved over to have a word with Arthur about the interruption but again thought better of it when he saw Eileen at his side patting him on the back.

Justice had been done without having to resort to a single pin or clay effigy.

Chapter Eight

Taboo or not Taboo

Normally the subject of sex does not feature very often as a topic of conversation in the wet fish queue on the market in the Straggling Town. This may, of course, be because the subject of fish is very often on our minds, and – as Arthur Wormwell had cause to remind me only the other day – fish don't do it, which is thought to be why the early Christians adopted this chaste creature as their symbol. When I pointed out that the existence of little fishes somewhat taxed the credibility of this theory, he was obliged to add, that if they did do it they managed to do it without touching, which made it all right for St Paul and his followers who we all know were very much down on sex. But then I wanted to know, even if fish didn't touch when they did it, what was to stop wicked thoughts from swimming into their minds? We both floundered for a while over this one and finally had to abandon the topic.

I suppose we're a bit like fish, too, those of us of Yorick age. Whatever our thoughts on the subject of sex, we generally prefer to keep them to ourselves. What people do and how they do it we prefer, quite properly, to leave to themselves. But who they do it with ... Ah, well, that's a different matter.

'She was with that footballer,' whispered Red Eileen, loud enough to be heard the full length of the Open Market.

It was the sort of day when the secrets of everybody's sexuality seemed likely to remain a secret. A raw, wet wind zipped off Black Moss reservoir, and the only discernible difference between the sexes seemed to be that on top of all the huddled overcoats, some were wearing headscarves and some were wearing flat caps. Which would be odd if it remained the only way of telling the difference.

'You know,' went on Eileen, above the sound of the canvas flapping on the market stalls, 'The one that got that nasty groin injury and had to retire early.'

But Hilda-the-Ton knew nothing about footballers, let alone their injuries. Unlike Eileen, she had not been married to a football-mad husband who had secretly sold her costume jewellery to finance a Sky satellite dish.

Then, Eileen suddenly revealed rather more of herself as far as sex was concerned.

Fleetwood Norman had been contravening the food hygiene regulations for as long as some busy-body bureaucrat had first introduced them. After placing your haddock – or whatever you fancied a bit of this week – on a piece of clean white wrapping paper, he proceeded to wrap the rest in newspaper. Until today, I'd only ever once heard of anyone objecting to this time-honoured way of dispensing fish, cooked or otherwise. And that was Bag o' Nails. He'd claimed that some highly toxic derivative of lead was contained in the newsprint which had been known to kill within hours. He'd been backed up by a highly neurotic nurse from the General Hospital who had reminded us all that people were in the habit of taking the daily paper to 'the smallest room in the house' to peruse it. Could Norman guarantee that the same newspaper he used to wrap his fish in hadn't also been there?

But, on this occasion it was not what may have been on the newspaper but what was in it which was being objected to. Fleetwood Norman was just in the process of transferring Eileen's pair of Manx kippers to the inside pages of a tabloid newspaper sporting a picture of a naked young lady looking as if it wouldn't be long before she'd be requiring the same frontal support that rendered obedient the quivering bosom of Hilda-the-Ton, when a voice like a siren stopped him.

'If you think I'm having my fish wrapped in them, you can think again!'

Now, naturally, Norman, a man of the world and used to the robust badinage of the wholesale fish market, didn't at first understand her, thinking it to be another complaint about the use of newspaper to wrap food.

'I'm the only one that's ever handled those,' he said, waving a very red and cold-looking hand in the direction of Tracy from Silsden, hobbies: step aerobics and snorkelling – as well as juggling, to judge from the pose she'd adopted. 'These are papers that never got sold.'

'That – picture,' burst Eileen, in a near apoplexy of moral outrage.

'I don't mind having mine in it,' piped up a very small man with watery eyes who was next in the queue. Eileen turned and killed him stone dead with one glance.

Fleetwood removed the offending articles and Eileen stalked off, fuming enough to resmoke her kippers.

'Bloody feminists,' muttered Fleetwood, and vented his fury on a cod roe which he filleted with all the finesse of a mad axeman.

But he was quite wrong. Eileen wasn't a feminist. We have no need of feminists in the Straggling Town. Women have always been on top. It is pure Darwinism. In the past, with six children to bring up and as many looms to run, and a husband as wet as one of Fleetwood's fish trays and more often than not drunk, only iron-willed women survived. And they bred daughters of similar mettle. Eileen was one such: a master-woman, beyond the giddiest dreams of Adolf Hitler. Who needs feminism when you're born with more testosterone in your knitting fingers than Arnie Schwartzenegger has in the whole of his iron-pumping, muscle-bound body? And sons? Well, the likes of Eileen saw to it that they were castrated at birth – metaphorically speaking – and any sexual feelings remained forever concealed under layers of rigorously-applied terror-stricken guilt.

But repression not only breeds guilt, it can also breed revolt, and a sexual revolution, of sorts, was being hatched even at that very moment in the Pack o' Lies pub.

Unfortunately, the landlord had recently passed on to do his Maker's bidding in cellars elsewhere. In their wisdom, the brewery had replaced Alf

with someone from out of town. Someone with modern ideas. He was a
furtive little whipper-snapper in tight shoes and a Paisley waistcoat from
Manchester called Ted. He may have been short but he had big ideas.
Entertainment every night to bring the punters in. No more of this
huddling in corners putting the world to right. No more conversation, the
curse of those who would have us all passive consumers. No more simply
sitting and dreaming in your cups of a better world, without bosses and
money troubles and where our football team carried off the European Cup
every season. All this was to be replaced by something called Fun Nights.
Brash and noisy with groups and karaoki: Elvis Presley look-alikes and
warbling wanabe Tina Turners, amplified to such a dog-howling intensity
that all sentient brain-activity, let alone speech, became impossible. And
there was something else. On Thursday nights he promised a 'Gentlemen's
Night.'

Some of the more worldly of us had heard of Gentlemen's Nights. Some
had even sampled their dubious delights. There had once been a pub over
Black Moss, a mildewed ill-frequented hole run for a few disgruntled
sheep-farmers, that tried to branch-out, lure people in from the town with
exotic dancers from Rochdale. But fatal injuries to drunken and inflamed
customers trying to negotiate the treacherous moorland roads on the way
home had severely affected attendances. And even girls from Rochdale
weren't prepared to take their clothes off for ten pounds, as many Baby-
chams as they could drink provided it was no more than two, and a packet
of crisps. But to suggest something like this in the middle of town, next
to the Twice-a-Night Bingo Club where wives and mums, and Eileen, may
have had their eyes down but whose bristling antennae for male treachery
never slept, was suicidal folly.

But the upstart Ted was blind to it. Deafened by his own discos, perhaps,
or simply the dreams of his till ringing in the lolly, he charged ahead like
a one-man Light Brigade with his glorious mission to liberate the poor
chained libidos of his customers. He had seen the haunted hungry look in
their eyes as they glanced up at Miss November on the Snap-off Tools
calendar which hung behind the bar. Particularly that Wormwell chap. Pity
he failed to notice that this was Arthur's permanent expression in the
presence of the new landlord and had more to do with our world being
taken over by money-grabbing little spivs like him than the sight of a few
pouting pin-ups.

Because it wasn't Red Eileen who intercepted the exotic dancer when
she stepped off the Todmorden bus that Thursday night clutching her
suitcase containing the rubber python, and with the help of £25 persuaded

her to get back on again and return to her two fatherless kids in Oldham.
It was Arthur Wormwell.

'Why did you do it?' I asked as we sat in the Pack o' Lies celebrating
the news that the new landlord had left to go back to Manchester where
people were more 'with it'.

'It's degrading,' he replied, staring reflectively at the new calendar of the
sun setting over Black Moss reservoir.

'Yes,' I agreed, 'to women.'

'To men as well,' he replied 'I don't want to see my mates leering and
tittering, in public. I know it goes on, but I don't want to see it.'

'Best kept hidden,' I said. 'Like fish.'

'Yes, like fish,' said Arthur.

Chapter Nine

Firm Foundations

*T*HERE was a mighty thwack of elastic like a gun going off. It came from the Knicker Stall on the Market where Hilda-the-Ton was testing out a pair of bloomers with all the thoroughness of a decathlete working out on his chest-expanders.

'By gum, that's stout stuff,' murmured Arthur.

Overhearing the remark, Hilda swung round like a Vickers tank, but not before Red Eileen, her shopping companion and structural foundations advisor, had herself swept into action with a handbag weighted like a medieval mace.

'Clear off from round 'ere, you perverts!' she hissed, the ghastly red gash of her lipsticked mouth outdoing the wildest efforts of a Hammer film make-up department.

It's an unwritten rule in the Straggling Town that the Knicker Stall is out of bounds to menfolk. For here those hidden mysteries which render obedient the wayward parts of stout and elderly matrons are laid out for the world to see. Bras stitched with catgut, so ample they would furnish an airsock for a small airfield, hang limp from the roof. Whalebones bristle dependably in a seemly sea of surgical pink. Even sugar-bag blue bloomers can still be purchased. But nothing frivolous, black or naughty in nylon; everything was as proper as a winceyette nightie advert in *The People's Friend*.

We scuttled away from the casbah of corsetry and made for the exit. In the foyer Arthur stopped to scowl at a poster advertising courses at the local College o' Knowledge. Nightschool classes included Bridge, Tofu Cookery and Well-dressing for Beginners.

'Waste of the rates,' he grumbled scornfully.

It was the gentrification of the masses he most deplored. The advertisers have a lot to answer for. He viewed the spread of Austrian blinds and conservatories as tantamount to the castration of the working class. Only a return to the raw vitality of straining whippets and heaving football kops could halt the insidious progress of the knife. Bridge and tofu was for tossers. Long live darts and suet pudding!

'But surely,' I argued. 'You can have nothing against people expanding their intellectual horizons.'

'Yes, I have,' he swore. 'It makes them miserable. Look.'

Slouching towards us at that very moment came Bag o' Nails, that megalith of human misery. His brow bore more dark clouds than a Bank Holiday weather map. What he didn't know about deadly pollutants and every detail of this planet's history of war and pestilence, you could write on the hem of a modern shirt lap.

'All right?' enquired Arthur jauntily.

This was a foolish salutation for Bag o' Nails. How could everything be all right in a universe primed for disaster, with the fuse already fizzing? Bag o' Nails cast a haunted, hunted look about him, from eyes sunken as shell holes.

Instead of waiting for the usual litany of woes, I pointed to the poster. 'Which one of these do you fancy enrolling for?' I asked chirpily. There were a few possibilities. Do-it-yourself Willmaking? Recognising symptoms of Ebola? The treatment of meteorite wounds?

'Fidding while Rome burns,' he grunted and nosed his way through the shoppers like a shark with toothache.

As we considered this contribution to the debate on the value of education, Eileen and Hilda hove into view. Ignoring us with the disdain Dracula might show for a plate of watercress, Eileen pointed to the poster and announced that she proposed to do soft-furnishing this year. Hilda, whose own portable soft-furnishings would have comfortably seated the Hallé Orchestra, nodded and, sending her voice up an octave in a bid to sound coy, intimated that Cake Decoration for the Calorie-conscious was more in her line. We removed ourselves, just in case Fair Sex Karate or Mud-Wrestling for Beginners caught their attention and sent them both into a sudden fit of aggression.

Over on the wet fish stall, Fleetwood Norman was unzipping the backbone from a dab as meticulously as a bodysnatcher removing an organ for spare-part surgery.

'Eleven years of full-time education for this,' brooded Arthur, scanning the assortment of stall-holders.

I tried to point out that we had no way of telling what was going on in their minds. Fleetwood may at that very moment have been reflecting on the exquisite symmetry of the DNA double helix.

'Come here, you thieving little bleeder!'

A voice like a works hooter erupted from the sweet stall, and a small boy in a silver-grey blazer sped past like a comet, clutching a tube of Smarties. I lunged to try and grab him but missed. Arthur, who was even closer, didn't move a muscle.

'Why didn't you stop him?' I remonstrated.

'Private enterprise,' grunted Arthur, shrugging at the rest of the stalls. 'A thief amongst thieves.'

Before I had time to consider this observation on our market economy, Eileen and Hilda-the-Ton emerged with the small boy pinned between them and wriggling like a hooked minnow. In the time it takes to shout 'lynch mob' they were surrounded by a score of stallholders.

It was not the boy so much as his uniform that was the object of indignation. It belonged to the latest opt-out from the state system, a private school charging fees of £1500 a term and with a waiting list of middle-class parents drooling over its league table ratings and eager to send their little white hopes through its exclusive gates to become brain surgeons. What were we to make of such villany amongst the ranks of the elite? Such a squirming little serpent in the meadows of parental hope?

'What did you expect in a country whose leaders steal the nation's family silver and fence it to their chums,' said Arthur, who had not yet got over the privatisation of the water boards. He thought the lad was probably just practising to become a cabinet minister. Eileen, blissfully unaware of what passes for abuse these days, was all for whipping down his well-pressed pants and smacking his bare bum. But it was Hilda, who as far as the stallholders were concerned, got to the real bottom of the matter.

'They're taught everything there is to know about computers and condoms these days, but nowt at all about right and wrong.'

'Firm foundations,' I mused, casting an admiring glance at the rock-solid outline of Hilda and thinking of the Cairngorms.

We turned away as the conversation turned towards the past and those old whalebones of morality: straps and canes, short sharp shocks and Sunday school, thumbscrews and gibbets. In fact, so powerful was the nerve-gas of nostalgia for the good old sadistic days of corporal punishment, that no-one noticed when the light-fingered scholar squirmed free of his captors and escaped via the knicker stall, where he helped himself to several yards of extra-strong knicker elastic. Enough to make catapults for the whole of his exclusive little class-mates.

Chapter Ten

Flying the Flag

THE UNION JACK on the town hall was flying at full mast for the Queen's birthday.

'I feel sorry for 'er,' said Red Eileen, nudging the woman in front of her in the wet fish queue who was dithering over the price of haddock.

Flags normally fly at half-mast from our town hall. In the Straggling Town we're more used to bereavement than the Co-op undertakers. We're a death certificate in stones and mortar. They shut down all our mills and pulled down our houses. Now it's all breeze block and queues at the Job Centre. When everybody else sniffs we expire from pneumonia. On the sign outside the town some wag has written, 'Twinned with Krakatoa'. People here don't expect things to last.

'She's the only one of them left, with any dignity,' pronounced The Red One.

There was a general murmur of assent from the queue, not because everyone necessarily agreed, but because it was Red Eileen who had spoken.

Everything she said was issued with a fierce challenge. It went with her fierce red outfit: red wellies, red coat, red rain-hood and red hair. When she spoke she threw back her head like a red hen about to peck you to death. She had pecked her way through three husbands.

'Royalty should behave different,' she asserted.

'There's such divinity doth hedge a king ...' mused Arthur Wormwell, who'd read his *Hamlet*.

The Red One swung round, winding a very small man with her shopping bag which contained five pounds of ready washed King Edwards.

'What's that?' she scowled.

Despite her dress there was nothing at all revolutionary about Eileen's political views. The red was more like war paint, designed to deter anyone who should dare to challenge the sovereignty of her views. But Arthur was different. You could tell by the fact that he wore an infamous Michael Foot donkey jacket. A symbol of the fustian hordes, drumming on the palace gates with lengths of lynch rope. Eileen turned to repel them single-handed.

'More than frying steak, cod, these days,' I chipped in.

This was a diversionary tactic to protect my chum. If there's one thing guaranteed to raise local passion more than the imminent collapse of the Establishment, it's the price of wet fish. Eileen's laser gaze shifted from Arthur and his donkey jacket to Fleetwood Norman.

'Over three pounds a pound,' stormed Eileen. It was a cool morning but I swear it was more than water-vapour which issued from her mouth.

'I'll bet they don't have to worry about the price of fish at Balmoral,' I whispered to Arthur with fatal misjudgment.

A whisper is about as much use as a commode in outer space in the Straggling Town. Everyone can lip-read. Red Eileen had sniffed sedition and homed-in on my remark.

'What's that?' she snarled.

It's no good trying to retaliate with someone like Eileen. Bend with the wind, is the best motto, a philosophy which has rewarded thousands of Straggling Town husbands, with flac-free lives and nightly refuge in the men-only bar at the Royal British Legion.

'I know you lot would like to get rid of her. You and that Richard Murdoch,' she went on. To correct her would have risked the marlin spikes of her finger nails.

'Then where would we be? she challenged, glowing like a struck match. Her eyes suggested the scorched bush of Australia, the arid suburban democracy of Ramsey Street. She may have had a point.

'Social parasites,' cried a voice from the second-hand magazine stall: it was a youth in a disbanded East German army greatcoat and a knitted bobble cap with a CND badge and sprouting a greasy ponytail. We all stood back simultaneously to be out of the line of Eileen's fire.

But nothing ever came. Instead, a small, quavering voice arose, as if one of Fleetwood Norman's sad, staring herrings had come back to life and started to sing. Everyone turned to look.

It was a small man we'd never seen before, small and old. He had that little boy-ish look some old men get as their life comes full-circle. His gaberdine mac was tightly belted, his shoes shone like anthracite. His neck was pink and scalped, shorn to the rim of his cap where his ears rested like scallops. He looked as if he'd just been turned out by his mum for a Whit walk, in the days when fun was all home-made and all the sweeter for being rationed.

'I lost this for her,' he announced, standing stiff and proud. With his good hand he pointed to his sleeve. It was empty, the cuff pinned neatly back to the shoulder with a safety pin. 'I'd do it again,' he added defiantly.

We swallowed. It was a hard swallow, to get down all our republican leanings.

'Peace, man! Peace!' sneered the foolish young man in the German greatcoat, raising two fingers in a mockery of a Churchillian salute.

But it didn't stop the blitzkrieg. Eileen shot towards him like a fireball and five pounds of King Edwards descended upon what remained of the communist bloc. The young man fled in panic.

Eileen resumed her place at the head of the queue. 'A pound of 'addock and two fish 'eads for our cat,' she ordered.

'Bet her cat eats sharks' heads,' whispered Arthur without moving his lips.

As we walked away from the market we were both thoughtful. 'My Grandma,' said Arthur suddenly, 'used to reckon that the Queen never went to the lavatory.'

'Then,' he went on, 'when she came on a royal visit in 1954, they put up five new toilets for her on the royal route. My uncle worked for the council and had to take them down afterwards.'

'What did your Grandma say?'

'She didn't believe it.'

One day, if the media get their way, there'll be nothing at all left to believe in. A journalist will visit Jodrell Bank and pick up a conversation between God and his mistress and sell it to *The Sun*. 'Gotcha God!' will be the headline.

But neither of us could shake off the thought of the one-armed man in the fish queue. Walking into a wall of screaming shrapnel armed only with a few verses of Rule Britannia and the memory of a picture of the monarch hanging on the elementary school wall. Who would we do it for today? The tarnished House of Windsor? Cabinet ministers who ditch their wives for their secretaries? Top judges who think nothing of spending £60,000 of our money on their wallpaper? Or would we do it for free speech and Red Eileen's right to terrorise the rest of us on the open market?

Just then a large chauffeur-driven limousine floated past, a pennant fluttering from the bonnet. In the back seat sat the Mayor in a gold chain with a tricorn hat and a red cloak lined with ermine. Arthur waved but the mayor didn't seem to notice.

'Stuck up beggar. Who does he think he is?' scowled Arthur.

It was Tommy Ridehalgh. He'd been to school with Arthur and me. What we could tell the world about Tommy would bring the B&Q wallpaper off the Mayor's parlour.

'We should sell our story to the local paper,' said Arthur spitefully.

But further down, the car had pulled up. As we drew level the window opened.

'Sorry lads,' said Tommy. 'I didn't spot you. Want a lift?'

We both gazed at Tommy's gold chain wistfully.

'No thanks,' said Arthur. 'It doesn't seem right.'

As the car purred off we both stood watching it. We might not have felt touched by divinity but we'd be liars if we didn't admit we both felt a bit proud. It's not everybody who's pally with a real live Mayor.

Chapter Eleven

Loads of Rubbish

*W*E WERE STANDING at the pie stall sampling the first of the day's batch of Pickup's pies: standing, like you do, nibbling into the rim of the crust with the pie carefully tilted backwards so as not to spill the juice, and blowing for all your worth at the molten contents to avoid a visit to the General Hospital for third-degree mouth burns; when there was such a hullaballoo from the traffic on the main road you'd have thought we were in the centre of Rome and not just a one-horse town in the middle of Pennine nowhere.

At first we ignored it, allowing nothing to interfere with the sacred ritual attached to the consumption of a fresh Pickup's pie. Ugly scenes have dramatically increased since the introduction of so-called traffic-calming measures into the town. The replacement of the tarmac with concrete cobbles may have slowed down the cars, but it's done nothing for the pulse-rate of the motorists. It's not just that the cobbles have an uncanny knack of loosening exhaust systems. It's the rather naive notion of our traffic legislators that people, whose lives have been cranked up to break-neck speed by the pressures of modern life will suddenly, just because they've been forced to drive more slowly by a road-surface that resembles the limestone pavements of Penn-y-ghent, slip into some sort of medieval mode of life, wind down the car window and strike up a conversation with a passer-by on the virtues of this year's elderflowers for wine-making. Anyone with their head screwed on right – that is, who doesn't work for a highway authority – will tell you that exactly the opposite tends to happen. Thwarted from passing through the town at their customary 50 miles an hour, drivers are overcome with a murderous desire to mount the pavement with their vehicle and chase pensioners, cripples and pregnant ladies in a mad effort to purge the environs of all legged life so that the highway people can come along and declare the area a pedestrian-free zone and introduce motorway regulations.

The cacophony of sounding horns became so loud that eventually we were forced to lay down our pies and send someone to find out what was going on. It appeared that the traffic was what is known as 'snarled up'. This does not refer, as it should do, to the expressions on the faces of the inconvenienced motorists, but merely that it was at a standstill. Arthur Wormwell, who's an old-fashioned romantic, had the quaint notion of rounding them all up, and by waving a fresh Pickup's pie in front of their nostrils, luring them into the Market to stand around with pies, hot black puddings and Eccles cakes and talk about gas-tar and tram lines and the winter of 1947 when they couldn't bury his great uncle Jack for fourteen weeks because of the snowdrifts. 'That'd help to slow life down for a bit,' he said. But, by this time the fug of exhaust fumes was so great that old ladies were beginning to collapse and flakes of stone were peeling off the old market cross. So we went to see what we could do.

It was all the fault of Jonas Metcalf, the Straggling Town's official scavenger. He'd been trying to cross the road with his home-made handcart, when the wretched cobbles had dislodged one of its pram wheels and the cart had shed its load.

Laid out before us were all the inadequacies of modern domestic technology. There were toasters which had enraged their owners by refusing to hand over their breakfasts until they were well and truly incinerated. Hairdriers which looked as though they'd been hit by lightening but had simply done what all hair-driers do when you're in a hurry to dry your hair on a Saturday night: they'd spontaneously combusted. There were cassette recorders that had taken to chewing tapes and spin driers that enjoyed shredding clothes. And, of course, there were television sets which had disappeared up their own dot.

Jonas, as usual, had culled all these defective articles from the backyards of their disappointed and frustrated owners. He timed his round to only minutes before the arrival of the dustbin men. He was a kind of pilot fish who swam ahead of the great yellow whale of the corporation dust cart, rescuing choice morsels before they disappeared for ever into its great steel maw.

No one minded Jonas. We all love a scavenger in the Straggling Town because at heart we are all scavengers ourselves. Hard times have taught us never to throw anything away except in anger. By way of rewarding our frugality, the planning authorities have located more boneyards, tips, incinerator plants, mad cow graveyards and secret toxic waste dumps in our locality than anywhere on the planet. This guarantees wealth for a few and premature death for the rest of us, a long tradition in the industrial north. But just what Jonas was able to salvage from the domestic jetsam of our brave new world, no one was sure. Some say he was able to extract valuable kryptonite from their innermost workings and fly by night over Pendle Hill. Others that he would return with them to his grimy caravan on the edge of the municipal tip and crouch over them and whisper new life into their errant spirits before cleaning them up and selling them off to the DHSS to furnish houses for the homeless.

Seeing the mess he was in, Arthur and I went over to give him a hand and return his loot to the cart.

'Dratted cobbles,' wheezed Jonas as he scrabbled around the road searching for whatever it was that held his pram wheel on. A pet-food salesman, his sales mission temporarily thwarted, nudged his car murderously closer. But Arthur picked up a television set and placing it in the middle of the road, pretended to switch it on.

'What are you doing?' I said.

'I thought all these motorists might want to watch it while they're waiting,' he replied genially. 'You see,' he went on, in his best Hyde Park Corner sermon voice, 'This is why they're all in such a flaming hurry. They rush around all day long just so that they can get home at night and slump in front of this thing. This is the pathetic carrot we all get when we finally reach the end of the stick.'

The motorists looked as though they'd reached more than the end of their sticks. Steering column knuckles were as white as a chicken's knee-caps.

'Neighbours. Eastenders. Big Break.' Arthur blithely laid all the BBC's glittering cultural jewels before his audience.

'That's what he must have thought when he threw it out,' said Jonas.

We both looked at the television. 'Who?'

'Bag o' Nails.'

We cleared the road as soon as we could. Perhaps Bag o' Nails was ill. Or, had he met some dazzling white dot somewhere on the road to close-down and this was his heroic stance against the cathode-ray menace? Perhaps we'd better pay him a visit. We may have something to learn from a man bold enough to cut himself loose from the cosy umbilical of TV and face the desolate tundra of life up north alone.

We called on him at the hour of least resistance. Just after tea, when the steak pudding and chips are lying heavily and the primal instinct to curl up in a cosy corner of the cave has been perverted into the modern urge to switch on Eastenders. That fatal moment which has the television executives chuckling inside their red braces as we reach for their visual barbiturates never to recover until it's too late and Boris Karloff arrives with the late night horror and the dawning realisation that the whole of the night has been lost.

Bag o' Nails' house in Disraeli Street looked like the grave. Not a light flickered. We knocked but there was no answer. We tried the door and it creaked open. Perhaps he was dead? Poisoned by his own bileful vision of the world? We pushed on through into the living room, where, suddenly, we were confronted by a huge shadow, hovering on the wall like a malign sickle.

'Merciful Heavens!' I cried, reaching for the bulb of garlic I keep in my breast pocket ready for encounters with the undead.

But it turned out to be nothing more than the silhouette of Bag o' Nails, hunched over a book at the table and reading by the light of a hurricane lamp to save on electricity.

'Are you all right?' asked Arthur when we'd recovered from our fright.

'As well as I can be with the Lord poised to rain down brimstone and fire upon this Gomorrah.'

Good lord, I thought. If this is what doing without television does to you, bring back Blankety Blank.

'What do you mean?' asked Arthur.

'We are the new Gomorrah,' boomed Bag o' Nails as the lamp growled like Stromboli.

What the Dickens had he been watching? Too much Ester Rantzen. Crown green bowling? It had tipped him over the edge.

'Pollution,' growled Bag o' Nails and raised a finger which looked as if it was suffering from Dutch elm disease.

'You're dead right there,' cried Arthur Wormwell with the almost hysterical enthusiasm you reserve to humour the dangerously insane before help arrives. 'Television is the worst kind of moral pollutant. All that sex and cookery programmes.'

'Come with me,' commanded Bag o' Nails, ignoring him and rising from his seat like the wrath of the Lord.

He took us down into the cellar.

It was like Hitler's command bunker. The whitewashed walls were full of maps with pins and coloured flags in them. So this was what he'd been doing instead of watching TV: planning an invasion of the North of England.

'Waste tips. Rubbish dumps. Landfill sites,' he boomed. 'All here on our doorstep. You are looking at an environmental time bomb.'

'But,' gasped Arthur, like a man reeling from a heavy dose of carbon monoxide. 'We thought it was your television. What happened to it?'

'Bust,' cried Bag o' Nails dismissively. 'But not to worry. I've got another.'

And then suddenly he glanced at his watch. His eyes lit up with what passed for joy in a megalith of misery.

'Now, if you don't mind, lads, I'll be getting back upstairs. We don't want to be missing Coronation Street, do we?'

Chapter Twelve

Westminster Comes to Town

*A*CAR plastered with placards nosed its way through the main street of the Straggling Town. A tannoy crackled with an accent not much heard in these parts, and when it was, it usually brought a few wrinkles to local noses.

'... underlines this party's commitment to a classless and undivided Bwitain ...'

'Tripe,' came a voice from the market, and it wasn't ordering cow's stomach.

We were having a by-election because of the recent death of our honourable member. It would be nice to report that he had passed away as a result of the rigours of his constituency duties. Perhaps pneumonia, cutting down bankrupt farmers from their barn beams. Or malnutrition, trying to survive off the pension like many of his constituents. Or as a result of being crushed under the wheels of a juggernaut, heroically protesting against the latest act of local environmental savagery, and dying in the ambulance due to the closure of the nearest community hospital, while surgeons haggled over the price of bandages.

But no. He'd keeled over after a surfeit of champagne and sewage-contaminated Morecambe Bay shrimps at a party convention. They'd attempted to revive him by showing him the next huge increase in MP's salaries but it was all in vain. He'd perished even before he'd time to submit his expenses.

But there are plenty more selfless idealists ready to take over the reigns of power, and just at that moment, the latest candidate revealed himself. Wearing a stick-on smile and holding out a hand as pale and mottled as a sick plaice, he homed in on the fish queue.

'Howace Pargeter, your pwospective pawliamentary candidate,' he announced, in the kind of lisp that single sex public boarding schools somehow manage to specialise in.

Two scrupulously permed and rinsed middle-aged ladies in cashmere coats, who had joined the queue in the vain expectation that Fleetwood Norman stocked monkfish amongst the kippers and roll-mops, literally fell upon the young man like two well-groomed cats on a fish head. You could hear the rasp of their eager tongues.

'Rest assured . . .' simpered one, caressing his large rosette.

'. . . you will always have our vote,' crooned the other, doing things with his outstretched hand David Mellor would never dream of being done to his feet, even in his wildest fantasies.

Howace was a young fogey. An earnest swot newly fledged from some exclusive hatchery for egg-heads. All intellect but no warmth. A high-flyer bitten by the frosts of the rarified upper atmosphere from where he would

forever look down upon his fellow man. His manner said it all: the curl of the lip, the smirk, the cold, dead eye, the assured, superior drawl. They all amounted to one thing: the elite.

Funny how we English seem to trust this type in politics. How we invariably vote for them at the expense of the down-to-earth, fire-in-the-belly chap. Is it because we are a nation of people who hate passion and make love with their socks on?

Me and Arthur Wormwell were both musing on this when our thoughts were interrupted by a voice like a rusty grappling iron.

'Tha dunt know owt about nowt. Tha's nobbut a kid.'

Our egg-head swivelled round like an owl. Had he been addressed in Sanskrit I've no doubt he'd have understood. But this was the language of one of his would-be constituents and he blinked in incomprehension.

The ageing cashmere sirens rushed to his defence, forming a protective wall of Eau-de-Cologne between him and the rude mechanical. It was Herbert Dobson, retired engine-man at Balaclava Mill, prize chrysanthemum grower and erstwhile paid-up member of the Communist Party.

'He says you don't know anything because you're too young,' explained someone.

'Wet behind t'ears,' came a more vernacular translation.

But Red Eileen, who had just arrived, sensing blood like a killer shark, had to throw in her two penn'orth.

' 'ow much is a pound of cod, then?' she demanded.

It was the cue for a challenging chorus of headscarves, flat caps and shopping bags to strike up.

'A bag o' coal? Smokeless?'

'Two hounces o' tongue. Cos we can't afford no more?'

'Gas and electric?'

'A decent burial? Hoak not chipboard? How much, then?'

The queue became animated, like a sea of mackerel, as it always did when the cost of living came up. The cashmeres fled the vulgar tide, leaving the would-be MP marooned.

He looked round desperately for the nearest cloistered quadrangle or West End wine bar, anywhere where such beastly matters were never discussed. But there was nowhere. Only grass-roots where nasty things come crawling out from under stones.

But help arrived in the hitherto unnoticed form of age and parliamentary experience. Detained at the tripe stall, where he'd received an impromptu lecture on elder and chitterlings by the owner, while his bodyguards bought meat pies, was a Very Senior Member of the Shadow Cabinet whose arrival in town had been kept secret for security reasons. (A small contingent of Irish tinkers was encamped on the edge of town and the file on Herbert Dobson was still open.) Just who he was nobody was sure, apart from the two cashmeres who returned on his heels in a swoon of fluttering mascara.

'Ah!' cried the VIP, like a housemaster breaking up a drugs ring in the bike shed with a quote from Plato: 'Healthy debate. The life-blood of democracy.'

A silence broke out, like war.

Undeterred, the VIP puffed out his rosette-strewn chest and went on in that patronising way that whitens knuckles north of the Trent.

'I see Horace has already introduced himself. A young man of impeccable credentials.'

Red Eileen looked as if she was ready to squeeze his credentials before handing them over to Her-on-the-tripe-stall.

'Cod,' she cried, like one of those hideous creatures whose grip cannot be released without breaking their jaws. ''Ow much is cod?'

Fleetwood Norman leaned over the back of his fish van and wet his lips like a spectator at a live garotting.

'Er, it's quite some time since I purchased any cod,' blustered the shadow minister as if he'd just dropped his notes under the dispatch box.

Eileen turned to the rest of the queue in triumph. 'See? They're out of touch!'

'Live in a different world!' nodded Hilda, shock waves passing down her stupendous frontage.

'Not fit to be elected,' pronounced Herbert Dobson, scowling as if he'd just seen an earwig crawl out of one of his chrysanthemums.

Question. What do a politician and a rat have in common? Answer: When cornered they both go on the offensive. Getting on in politics means learning never to say you're sorry.

'Now, look here,' puffed the Very Important Person. 'Our party's record on inflation is second to none. Don't let anyone tell you we don't care about prices. We do care.'

Eileen and Hilda were being hectored. No man has ever hectored Eileen and Hilda and lived. The two security men stopped thinking of meat pies and closed in on their leader.

'You don't care about me.'

The voice was dry and feathery, sounding as if it had been stored for years in the corner of a chicken shed. Its owner was Jonas Metcalf our local rag-and-bone man, a dusty, dishevelled figure in third-hand rags and battered trainers from which his toes peeped out like a family of black mice.

Jonas didn't have a house but made do with an old caravan on some derelict land behind the supermarket. But plans for an extension to the supermarket carpark had recently led to an eviction notice. This was the essence of Jonas's wounded appeal to the VIP.

As the man from Westminster heard the story his eyes were all over the place. It wasn't difficult to see that his mind was already speeding chauffeur-driven down the M6 away from this wretched place for ever. Jonas's appeal looked as doomed as the bluebottle that had just settled on Fleetwood Norman's prawns and with the help of a descending fish slice was about to be reunited with the great Beelzebub.

But then something unexpected happened. Percy Smallcroft, who was covering the campaign for our local paper leaned over and whispered something into the eminent man's ears. The wandering eyes settled and narrowed. Percy, a hack as shrewd as he was odious and who liked to sell his pictures to the national papers to finance his devotion to Braithwaite's bitter, had got him interested. The next thing, the party was moving off, 'To inspect Jonas's domestic arrangements,' as Percy put it.

Most of us followed – like you do when something interesting happens in a town that can be as boring as peeling carrots. Soon, we were all squeezing into Jonas's caravan at the back of the carpark.

It was a sight to carry to the grave. A black interior stuffed with the festering jetsam of the consumer society and lapped by the smoke from Jonas's coke stove. And there in the middle, perched on a tin of used sump oil, a would-be minister of state in a Savile Row suit, wondering what on earth to do with a battered enamel mug of tea and a ginger nut that had just been handed to him out of an old paint tin. His protege close-by earnestly absorbed what he could of this exercise in meeting the people, while Jonas sat in a battered armchair piled high with mildewed cushions, holding court like the king of the Underworld.

Meanwhile, Percy bustled about rearranging commodes, lavatory seats and bed-pans, or whatever other salubrious objects lay at hand to enhance the spectacle, and took pictures for all he was going to be worth.

Of course, within a fortnight Jonas's caravan had gone and the bulldozers were in levelling the land for the carpark. But the VIP's stock has never been higher amongst his colleagues in the party. He's still regaling his dinner guests over the creme brulée with his account of how he survived the Dickensian nightmare of life amongst the northern savages. And millions of tabloid readers now rest easy in their beds knowing that politicians really do care and are in touch with the people they represent.

≈   *Chapter Thirteen*   *≈*

Splendour in the Glass

*T*HERE IS A MOMENT, somewhere during the second pint of Old Rapture, which can truly be described as beatific. Now, I am aware that such a remark may arouse cries of moral indignation from some of you – those for whom drink is the Devil's web, and those who have never had the good fortune to taste Old Rapture. It is, nevertheless, in my experience, true. Poets and philosophers, saints and visionaries, have those rare and blissful moments when the baffling pieces of the cosmic jigsaw suddenly spring together and their own place in the anarchic and alien universe suddenly becomes shiningly clear. Well, for me and other benighted souls in the Straggling Town, these moments occur regularly while standing at the bar of the Poet and Peasant Working Men's Club with that second pint of Old Rapture in our hands.

'By gum, this is something special,' cried Arthur Wormwell, the end of his nose well-annointed with creamy froth.

All the petty irritations of the day had suddenly fallen away, like snow shuttering off a roof. That hard shell, vital to the defensive armoury of modern life, quietly dissolved, and the people around us – Bag o' Nails

58

moping at the other side of the bar (he will drink stout), the landlord, gloomily inspecting his till – became comrades I would die for. I even managed a smile for the odious hack Percy Smallcroft who had bummed a drink off me and was about to leave without buying one back. The elixir of Old Rapture had again worked its magic.

'We can't go on like this,' grumbled Jack Lonsdale, the bar steward, slamming the till drawer with a crash. 'In another month this place will be shut.'

Reality in all its chilling sobriety returned like the morning after. The thought of no Poet and Peasant was an anathema. To be consigned to finding a replacement watering-hole was to be left to wander a purgatory of modern nightmares: of plastic theme pubs reeking of chips; of video palaces throbbing with decibels; or, at the very best, some cosy but alien hearth before which you will forever remain a stranger. But worst of all to lose our treasured Old Rapture served up with its special brew of seriousness and wit, poetry and profanity, which makes up the conversation of the Poet and Peasant Working Men's Club. Oh, woe and alack!

'Just look at it! Wednesday night! It used to be heaving. Now, it's dead as a pint of …' Here he mentioned a brand of lager which through advertising has become a household name, along with other household detergents.

It was true. We were a sorry company of exiles already. Made to feel, by sheer lack of numbers, that we were some furtive band of outlaws cut-off from the mainstream of decent society by our vice. Justly reviled by churchgoers and chief constables alike. Why weren't we at home in the bosoms of our families? Watching television movies about rape, murder and drug addiction, like normal people? I took a long draught of Old Rapture and reconciled myself to the hopelessness of our case.

Jack Lonsdale began to list the various demands on his customers' finances that could be keeping them away. But the cost of summer holidays and Benidorm sangria were still too far away to influence the club's takings.

'Jeff's been to Calais for the day,' announced Bag o' Nails in Day of Judgement tones.

It was not at all clear to minds somewhat unfocussed by the lotus-like qualities of Old Rapture what effect one man's day trip to France could have on the imminent closure of our cherished watering hole. Bag o' Nails was content to remain inscrutable.

'Calais,' he requested, and then added cryptically, 'He hired a van.'

Cheap beer! He's been buying duty-free beer! It hit us like a price-rise.

'Foreign muck,' nodded Bag o' Nails gravely. 'He came round to my house trying to sell me some. He's got enough to refloat the *Titanic*.'

Maybe he meant sink. But then, since the *Titanic* was already well and truly submerged, perhaps he didn't. It was enough for Bag o' Nails just to mention the great disasters of our time in his conversation. His mind was a huge reservoir of human misfortune which regularly burst its banks. The current disaster seemed to overwhelm Jack Lonsdale.

'The ungrateful beggar,' he swore.

'I can't understand people wanting to drink at home, especially nasty foreign lager. I'd rather do without,' I said.

'Escapism,' replied Arthur, handing over his glass to be refilled. 'A few cans of lager is the quickest way out of the Straggling Town for some.'

'And the cheapest, it seems,' added Jack Lonsdale ruefully.

We grew silent as, with a series of ecstatic squeaks from the handpump, we watched him ease the liquid into the glass. The chaos of malty bubbles settled into a ruby richness of breathtaking clarity. The bar lights shone through like sunlight through stained glass.

But the thought of the loss of our club had clouded our thoughts.

Just then, who should walk in but the man-mountain himself, Jurassic Jeff.

'For God's sake, give us a decent pint,' he growled. 'My throat's like a chemical dump.'

But Jack Lonsdale refused to move. 'It can burn in Hell along with the rest of you before you'll get another drink in here,' he snarled.

Now to deny Jurassic Jeff is rather like failing to give way to a goods train on an unmanned level-crossing. But the collision never came. Instead, Jeff sagged like his own weight in marshmallow. I have seen this happen before when men have been denied Old Rapture, when a barrel has run dry and its replacement, not having reached the peak of perfection must remain a day longer in the yeasty dark for the consumption of the miracle. Then I have watched grown faces crumple like children's and eyes fill with tears.

But when confronted with the alleged attempt to ruin the Poet and Peasant through the sale of contraband lager, Jurassic Jeff started to laugh.

'Sell that stuff? I couldn't give it away. Mark my words, anybody that's tasted it will be queuing to come back here for some decent ale.

He was right. Friday night was packed. Like a revivalist meeting. So much Old Rapture we thought we were in Heaven.

Chapter Fourteen

A Host of Golden Pickup's Pies

*T*HE WARM WEATHER had brought out some rare sights in the Straggling Town. There was Hilda-the-Ton sailing down the main street in a floral dress of giant pink and white petunias looking for all the world like a garlanded Indian elephant that had broken loose from an oriental festival. At her side, half her size but no less awesome, Red Eileen, the natural fire of her belligerent cheeks stoked to a dangerous crimson by the heat – and this, despite the furious wafting of a flamenco dancer's fan which distinctly bore the words, 'A present from Torremolinos'. Male paunches, trembling tributes to a lifetime's devotion to Braithwaite's bitter, sagged from straining T-shirts, while pale knees, the colour of blanched celery, and that last saw air in the top class at Corunna Road Junior and Infants Mixed, peeped shyly out from the folds of baggy shorts. Even Arthur Wormwell had been persuaded to grudgingly cast off his woollen vest and exchange it for a

Hawaiian shirt his wife had or-dered from her catalogue, and which had such a vertiginous pat-tern that Jimmy Capstick had fallen off his bar stool at the Poet and Peasant Working Men's Club when he first set eyes on it. And six or seven freckles had begun to merge on Arthur's face in a bid to offer some kind of united front against the onslaught of the sun. Colour, normally bleached from our lives here in the Straggling Town by months of incessant rain and clouds as grey as pumice, had made a spectacular reappearance, and with it had come a sense of

well-being unknown since Geoff Hurst sealed England's victory over West Germany in the World Cup.

There were some exceptions: there always is in a town where pessimism is elevated to the status of a religion. Fleetwood Norman was complaining bitterly about the plunging sales of haddock and the proliferation to plague proportions of fish-eating bluebottles in the vicinity of his mobile fish van. Bag o' Nails refused to step out, convinced that if there was a hole in the ozone-layer admitting lethal doses of gamma radiation onto our heads, it would be bound to appear directly over the Straggling Town. Percy Smallcroft, odious doyen of hacks and chief reporter of the *Straggling Town Examiner*, complained that it was too hot to work, an activity he'd never been known to indulge in, if you exclude collecting gossip from the taproom of the Pack o' Lies pub. And Jonas Metcalf was so snowed under with broken-down fridges his scrapyard began to look like a distribution centre of Igloo Foods.

The cobbles shimmered, the tarmac bubbled, smoke hung over the moortops from countless moorland fires. It wasn't like the Straggling Town at all, but more like somewhere in Spain or Italy – if you ignored the rows of grey terraces, their sash windows winking in the sunlight. And to add to the sense of unreality, what should suddenly appear in our midst but an air-conditioned luxury stratocruiser coach full to the luggage racks with camera-toting American tourists.

At first we thought it must have been a scoop for our new Director of Tourism, Austin Perry, BA (Hons), Theme Park Studies, the University of Sneckerton Pullover. He'd been trying his hardest to get the Balaclava Street Shoddy Mill onto the Grand Tour for foreign tourists, neatly sandwiched between Stratford-upon-Avon and the Lake District. He must have succeeded, bringing millions of US dollars into the town and its one and only bed and breakfast place.

This was not quite true. What had happened was that the coach driver, grown giddy from the smoke from countless Havana cigars and the ceaseless chatter of Prozac-popping Pasadena mommas, had turned prematurely off the M6, and taking the heat and smokehazed hills of the Pennines to be the Lake District, had arrived in the town and disgorged his eager passengers. And here they were, waving their copies of Wordsworth and Beatrix Potter, descending on the market demanding to know if the blood-stained carcasses hanging from the roof of the butcher's were relatives of Peter Rabbit or whether Bag o' Nails, who was gloomily toying with a bag of Pontefract cakes, was a leech gatherer.

Word of their arrival spread to the town hall with as much speed as news of a free lunch. In no time, Austin Perry, with an entourage of handpicked heritage sirens – the biggest and bounciest girls from the typing pool – arrived on the market to urge them to pay a visit to the Mother Moleseed Museum of Witchcraft, or try the Sackcloth Weavers' Heritage Trail along the oil slick that passes for a canal. But the Americans, realising at last that they were still 60 miles from Dove Cottage and in a part of the country more noted for its tripe and onions than hosts of golden daffodils, were just about to reboard their coach when who should sally forth from a visit to the pie stall but our own answer to Great Gable, Jurassic Jeff.

Could it have been the union-jack shorts which caught the attention of our trans-Atlantic cousins, bringing a sudden pang of regret that they ever opted for independence? Or was it the sight of his naked torso tattooed

with the claret and blue coat of arms of his beloved football team? Perhaps it was simply the sight of anyone so closely resembling Piltdown man managing to walk upright and still hold a pack of lager and a bag full of Pickup's pies which so astonished them. Or was it that, at that moment, he chose to stop, remove one of the famous pies, and, nibbling a hole in the crust like a fastidious harvest mouse, throw back his mighty head and slurp the juices with a noise like a parched camel that's just arrived at a desert watering hole.

'Gee, man! What's he got?' gasped one of the tourists whose stomach was still complaining over the motorway breakfast of soggy croissants and stewed coffee.

Now I've never known our town being noted for any entrepreneurial zeal. To us a market place is somewhere where you meet up with old chums and have a good natter, and profit is counted less in cash and more in the rich warmth of human contact. But today, Lady Hacksaw herself would have been proud of us.

Suddenly our American visitors were swamped. Her-from-the-Tripe-Stall emerged like a South Sea Islander welcoming the ship of Fletcher Christian. Only instead of flowers, she bore round her neck a garland of shining blackpuddings. Fred Pickup, who was bringing a tray of freshly-baked pies to the Cosy Cafe, just happened to make a slight detour to bring the steaming delicacies within nostril distance of the visitors. The effect was as dramatic as it was instantaneous. Casting aside their copies of Wordsworth and drooling like mastifs, they followed Fred into the cafe. Laid out before them was a banquet of local viands to bring tears of withdrawal to the eyes of any Weightwatcher. Doris had conjured up some of her famous rag puddings – suet nests of bubbling steak and kidney. Fred's pies were set sail in a sea of bobbing marrowfat peas and annointed on their way with copious blessings of brown sauce. There were the esoteric delights of stew and hard, tripe and elder sozzled in vinegar, and enough parkin and Eccles cakes to stock a street party. And bottles of Braithwaite's bitter, and even a special brew of Old Rapture, found their way onto the tables, poured into plastic cups and concealed because the cafe had no drinks licence. Even the ladies from Pasadena grew silent as America ate and drank deep of Straggling Town hospitality.

Austin Perry was furious. He hated it. He liked his food served up in the same way as his heritage: boil in the bag. And he didn't like us locals stealing his thunder. When the Americans emerged from the market, burping happily into the afternoon sunshine, he did his level best to ensnare them into one of his dusty museums and along his threadbare heritage trail. His career depended upon it – his unctuous passage to Chief Executive Officer. But they ignored him. In the time it takes to shout 'Have a nice day, now!' they were back onto their coach and off on their way to snooze their way around the Lake District.

'Now that's what you call heritage,' said Her-from-the-Tripe-Stall, rubbing salt into the wound. 'They'll remember that meal long after they've forgotten Ann Hathaway's cottage.'

Austin Perry bit his lip and slunk off back to his desk at the town hall, leaving the market to murmur away in the heat like a crowd of happy insects, as everyone counted their takings.

Chapter Fifteen

A Political Hot Potato

*B*ONFIRE NIGHT at the Poet and Peasant Working Men's Club is always an occasion for heated political controversy and there's always a whiff of sedition in the air long before anyone smells woodsmoke. It may be because, here in the Straggling Town, so far from the seat of Government and our needs generally ignored by MPs, a secret admiration for Guy Fawkes still survives. Anyone prepared to blow up the Houses of Parliament – and this long before the cost of prescriptions rose about £5 and the old age pension was barely enough to feed an anorexic supermodel – has our tacit approval. In fact, every year we honour Guy Fawkes by refusing to burn him. Instead we prepare likenesses of living figures and fill their pockets with paraffin. It is a community's collective revenge on those we feel have done us wrong. One year we had Margaret Thatcher unmistakable in tinfoil. At the time of the pit closures we had Michael Heseltine with a head full of blazing straw. This year we thought we might have Tony Blair, to see if, like the Cheshire cat, his smile was last to disappear. Or Peter Mandelson upon a dome of wood. It's all innocent fun let me assure the members of MI5 who, I'm told, and for reasons quite beyond me, have taken to listening in to our telephone conversations.

The question of the Guy had still not been resolved the day before the bonfire. Arthur and I were busy dragging brushwood across the fields to the wasteland at the back of the club. It's harder these days to get kids to help you gather plotwood than it is to persuade them to wash behind their ears. So there we were busying away while the bonfire took shape like a giant triffid. The weather was glorious, with the chestnut trees ablaze with autumn sunlight and the rowan berries glinting like rubies. Like overgrown kids we scrabbled about in the undergrowth snaring our pants on brambles and fighting over late blackberries. We sat in the gathering leaf mould underneath the great beech trees as the leaves fell like fat, yellow tears, and a nostalgia for the past flooded over us.

We talked about how, as lads, we used to have to guard our bonfires because of the Garretys. They were Catholics, just like Guy Fawkes, and used to try and sneak up in the night and set fire to our bonfire prematurely. And, of course, we used to try to do the same to theirs. We talked about the dens we always used to build in the middle where we used to sit and read comics by candlelight, a business so risky, when you consider all the old sacks and newspapers that surrounded us, that once, Peter Ramsbottom, so absorbed by the latest machinations of the Mekon in *The Eagle*, forgot to notice that his candle had fallen over and we had an early bonfire that year without any help from the Garretys. For old time's sake we even built a hollow in the centre of this year's bonfire and, checking that no one was looking, crawled inside and sat there for a while feeling self-conscious and a bit silly.

But Arthur was still troubled about the Guy. It was his responsibility because he was the only one who got the serious newspapers, and stuffing a Guy is one of the few sensible uses for all those sections and supplements. We were busy discussing possible local candidates for incineration as we dragged our wood along the lane behind the club when a large car stopped and winding down the window someone shouted 'Oy!' So complete had been our regression into childhood that our first instinct was to drop our wood and run. But it wasn't long before this changed to indignation. Who was this who was addressing us like a stray dog?

It was the bumptious money-maker and waste contractor, Councillor Horace Slack. He'd been responsible for opening up more landfill sites in the Straggling Town that the Kaiser's artillery had managed along the Western Front, all with the mysterious approval of the planning committee of which he happened to be chairman.

A head, round and hairless and shining like a well-greased baking potato addressed us from the driving seat.

'I'll send thee a wagon load o' stuff for that bonfire o' thine,' he yelled in his no-nonsense, I'm-the-salt-of-the-earth-and-don't-you-forget-it way that nauseated most people who knew that he lived like a lord in a mock castle he'd had built well up-wind from his waste-tips that choked the rest of us and on which his money grew like fungus.

'It'll probably be a consignment of nuclear waste,' I said as he drove off. But Arthur was silent. The worried frown had melted from his face.

Bonfire night was always a cracker. The club's recreation committee set aside a generous sum for fireworks. Our pyrotechnical expert was Arthur's cousin, Eric, who worked as a lab technician at the local high school and had a reputation for unscheduled explosions. Today he'd spent all morning digging holes for something he sinisterly referred to as his 'mortars'. Tottering along behind him, our only First World War veteran, 'Salient'

Sam Wilkinson, was on hand to offer ancient tactical advice and keep a look out for snipers. Eric always kept the nature and origins of his fireworks a secret, but we knew he had suppliers deep within the People's Republic of China because he'd been seen borrowing 'Teach Yourself Chinese' from the lending library.

All day long, Red Eileen, Hilda-the-Ton and Her-from-Next-Door busied themselves preparing the bonfire supper. By mid-afternoon the most sublime smell arose from the kitchen at the back of the club. It came from an old metal clothes boiler, brimful of a thick and muttonous stew whose gelatinous properties, enhanced by the addition of several cow-heels, had been known to seal the lips, literally, of the most garrulous club members. Tins of home-made parkin baked to ancient and secret recipes and lots of plot toffee had been arriving all day. By nightfall the atmosphere was fizzing like a fuse.

After a few drinks at the bar – to steady the nerves ready for some of the more raucous fireworks, you understand – we all trooped outside to the bonfire. The guy was already positioned on top and draped with a

blanket ready to be exposed only at the moment the fire was lit. There was the smell of paraffin being applied and the spurt of matches.

'So, who've you got this year?' boomed an unexpected voice from the darkness. It was Councillor Horace Slack.

He didn't have long to wait for an answer. To a woosh of blazing brushwood that lit up the whole bonfire, Arthur yanked the rope that held the blanket. Perched atop the hungry flames was a guy with a head round and hairless and shining like a well-greased potato.

'Why, you   ' roared the inspiration for the effigy. But the rest of his words, like his business dealings, never came to light. For at that moment, the first of the People's Republic mortars, having been fitted with a secret device to seek out bloated capitalists, veered from its planned trajectory and smote him full in the corporation – or what would have been the Corporation were we not now a Borough Council. Bag o' Nails, who was standing next to him, refused to put out the flames with his drink, saying afterwards that it would have been a criminal waste of good beer. Instead, there was no shortage of willing hands to unceremoniously wrap the civic dignitary in the blanket and roll him around on the ground for a good deal longer than was needed to put out the flames. He was finally released, smoking yet unscathed, but so dizzy he had to be prevented from walking straight into the bonfire and joining his charred likeness.

After such a good start the bonfire couldn't fail to be anything but a roaring success, or, as Arthur Wormwell said, 'It couldn't have gone better if we'd plotted it.'

≈≈   *Chapter Sixteen*   *≈≈*

Daedalus Wormwell

*A*NYONE in the Straggling Town with an allotment will tell you how hard it is here to grow decent carrots. The cold and sticky clay left behind by those glaciers that ground out our Pennine valley is too unrelenting for the questing root and they come out bent and twisted like the Devil's tail. And it's the same with people. The tender, rarified soul who cultivates the artistic life is unlikely to be found mincing his way up our main street clutching a blue carnation and reciting the poems of Baudelaire. The climate and conditions just aren't right for that sort of thing. Rude tongues would mock and jeer at such pretentions. A lifetime spent with a stubborn chin thrust out against the wind and rain raising sheep on a hill farm, or chained to the mechanical grindstone of the mill weaving cotton or hewing stone from dripping obdurate quarries, toughens the soul, and like a butterfly upon a wheel, breaks the artistic spirit. Practical virtues take the place of imaginative flights of fancy and the human soul remains grounded, like a Wellington boot in mud. Since those queer frail birds, the Bronte sisters, flew on, few have remained to sing the song of the spirit of these moorlands.

And even today, when life has been made easier, when, instead of struggling to raise sheep you can let your land to a renewable energy consortium for a windfarm or open it up to waste tips, and sit back in comfort raking in the rent; when the grinding mills are all cosy retail parks and the only time people sweat is over an Indian take-away; even now, we remain stubbornly practical and highly suspicious of what we are pleased to call the arty-farty. If Ibsen or Shakespeare comes to the Mechanics Institute at the expense of a few extra wheelie bins on the rates, voices are raised and horny fists thumped as no-nonsense councillors with pot ducks up their front-room walls want to know why we can't have more Chubby Brown or Bernard Manning. All right, we have our own theatre now, but stuck out of town next to the landfill sight, the right place for art and all that rubbish.

But nevertheless, just as carrots will struggle to grow whatever their resultant shape, the creative spirit will not be stifled, even here in the Straggling Town, the home of the working ferret and the chip butty. The candle of culture splutters to stay lit in many a dark cloister and draughty attic.

But the servant of art must sometimes pay a high price for loyalty to his Muse. We need to look no further than the blindness of Milton, the deafness of Beethoven, and, when we were left to reflect upon such matters at the bar of the Poet and Peasant Working Men's Club, what we began to fear was the approaching madness of Arthur Wormwell.

Arthur had not been out for a drink for a week. A whole barrel of Old Rapture had been consumed during that period. And an excellent barrel it had been, provoking mirth and tears in equal proportions, the tears always coming at closing time when we had to leave behind our glasses. It also produced much singing on the way home and several calls to the police by some of the elderly residents of Balaclava Street – dry, joyless folk who had signed the pledge at Junior School and lived a benighted life ignorant of the blessings of the hop. And after one session, Rufus Moorhead had failed to arrive home at all on to his farm on Blackedge Moor, having spent an untroubled night in a ditch, snoring loud enough to excite the attention of a female badger who, convinced that she had at last found a mate, snuggled up beside him and kept him warm until dawn.

We'd paid Arthur a call to tell him what he was missing but he was not to be found at home. We'd finally tracked him down to a lock-up garage in Garibaldi Gardens. But no amount of pleading would persuade him to open the doors. What on earth was he up to? Neighbours had attested to seeing a strange flickering light in the night, and soon rumours were circulating that Dr Frankenstein was in there assembling a monster from the spare parts of council officials who had passed away at their desks through lack of work.

Then, the next evening, as we returned from the club after a particularly fatiguing time judging the merits of two new rival brews, we caught sight of a shadowy figure making his way along the shed wall of the derelict Providence Mill. It was Arthur Wormwell and he was pulling his home-made trolley, the one with the pram wheels he'd had since he was a lad and used to bring coke from the gas works.

'We'll follow him,' whispered Jimmy Capstick. 'See what he's up to.' So we did.

We saw him slink into the scrapyard at the far end of the old engine house where the mill dam had been. Here was a mountain of old looms and other broken up bits of textile machinery. An elephants' graveyard, all that was left of our once-mighty cotton industry, stored now for its worth in scrap and insurance against the day when the cunning Hun might go on the rampage again and cut off our imports of iron ore.

'What the Devil's he up to?' growled Bag o' Nails. 'There's Alsatians in there. He'll be torn to pieces.'

But the only guard dog in there was as deaf as a cobble and had been fast asleep all night and remained so when Arthur emerged again ten minutes later, the pram wheels protesting under the weight of scrap metal that was being half-inched.

'I didn't know he was that desperate for money,' whispered Jimmy Capstick. 'We could have had a whip-round.'

By the time we caught up with him again the garage doors in Garibaldi Gardens were once more firmly locked, and this time we saw for ourselves the flicker of blue light.

'He's welding summat,' cried Bag o' Nails. 'That's what he's doing.'

But no amount of knocking on the doors would bring him out to offer an explanation and soon we were all trailing off home to bed as mystified as ever.

The following night as we sat in the club nursing our pints, the door burst open and in dashed Arthur. His appearance confirmed our worst fears. His face was flushed and blackened, apart from where his welding goggles had left a pale outline round his eyes which shone and danced wildly.

'I want you to help me,' he blurted.

'Of course we will, lad,' said Herbert Entwistle kindly, who'd done a spell as an attendant at Calderstones. 'Come and sit yourself down and have a pint.'

'No!' cried Arthur. 'It will be light, soon.'

Vampires, we all thought at once. The vampires have got him.

'Meet me back at the garage when you've supped up,' he urged, and was gone as fast as he'd arrived.

We took a supply of bottles to steady our nerves. Back at the garage we had to knock on the door again. The excited face of Arthur appeared at a gap before hurrying us in. Inside it was pitch dark and we hovered nervously near the threshold. What on earth had he got for us?

'This is it,' he cried and triumphantly switched on the light.

'Hell's bells!' cried Bag o' Nails, thunderstruck.

Rising to the garage roof was a tangled mass of cogs and wheels, rods and axles, assembled in the shape of a giant figure. Some terrifying mechanical robot. But, in the way the arms were outstretched and the hollow eyes raised heavenwards, there was a pathetic, mute appeal which rendered it touchingly human.

'What is it?' asked Jimmy Capstick, whose throat had gone dry despite the fact that he was holding an opened bottle in his hand.

'It is us,' cried Arthur Wormwell. 'Mankind. Trapped by the machine until we have become it. Soulless, manipulated consumers. Cogs enmeshed in the ruthless machine of capitalism.'

'Blimey,' cried Jimmy Capstick. 'He could be right.'

Convinced of his genius, we were ready to do his bidding.

For the next hour we pushed and grunted our way under the weight of Arthur Wormwell's creation as far as the square in front of the library. There, next to the Straggling Town's only other work of public sculpture, the weathered and pigeon-stained likeness of Alderman Amos Slack, we erected it.

The next morning, the Straggling Town came to a standstill as everyone arrived to inspect it. Rumours had soon spread that in the night we had been visited by aliens and this was their calling card. But when Arthur Wormwell appeared, to measure the effects of his creation on his fellow citizens, he felt obliged to correct this misapprehension. Standing on a bench he explained the true meaning of the work.

'Behold!' he railed. 'Look upon yourselves. You are automatons.'

Nobody had the remotest idea what he was on about and everyone thought he was drunk. But Red Eileen, resenting any suggestion that she was not in charge of her own affairs, moved menacingly towards him brandishing a large ham shank she'd just bought off the market. An ugly scene was only averted by the arrival of civic authority in the portly form of Councillor Ormerod Tinniswood, Chairman of the Libraries and Arts Committee. Alien artifacts were all right. But works of art, without the official approval of his committee, and of a dangerously radical nature, could not be tolerated. In the time it takes to shout, 'The Philistines are upon us!' the metalwork was removed in a council dustcart and now lies under several hundred tons of domestic rubbish on the council's landfill site. A layer of cold and sticky clay covers it and should guarantee that nothing like that ever grows in this soil again.

Chapter Seventeen

Bag o' Nails and the Angel of Death

$\mathcal{T}$HE PRESENCE of any widespread pre-millennium tension has so far failed to show itself in the Straggling Town. The prospect of a wholesale computer breakdown does not alarm us. If the banks and building societies collapsed tomorrow most of us would breathe a sigh of relief. Our money is usually kept hidden under a loose floorboard well away from the prying eyes of the Inland Revenue. And who would not welcome the non-arrival of all those impudent demands for money for a few basic necessities like heat, light and a reasonable supply of fresh water. We're told that the emergency services may be reduced to chaos, but they generally take so long to arrive up here in the Straggling Town that we've usually managed to sort things out ourselves long before they put in an appearance. We can fight fires, deliver babies and set up a hue and cry after a shop-lifter because folk learnt to do that sort of thing long before people in uniforms came on the scene. And as for what the council provides for the king's ransom they charge for rates, no one would notice if they stopped tomorrow, the services they offer are so pathetic.

No one is getting excited about going down to London to visit Peter Mandelson's dratted dome because we can recognise a mish-mash of public relations nonsense when we hear about it. And in any case, rather like Blackpool Pleasure Beach, it's all got too expensive for families trying to make ends meet on a minimum wage. We'll no doubt be arranging our own celebrations nearer the time, with a good family day at the Poet and Peasant Working Men's Club and a tasty home-made meat and potato pie supper and a brass band, and all for nothing.

We're wise and realistic enough here in the Straggling Town to know that the arrival of the beginning of the next thousand years isn't going to alter things much. The rich will continue to get richer at the expense of the poor. The meek will still not inherit the earth but only get trampled all over by the pushy. Rupert Murdoch and supermarkets will get bigger and greedier and the latter's bread will get worse. Red Eileen will have to put even more red henna on her hair to cover up the grey bits. Hilda-the-Ton will get even closer to weighing a ton. Percy Smallcroft, our resident hack from the *Straggling Town Examiner*, will continue to get drunk in the Pack o' Lies when he should be reporting the news and how many back-handers continue to be passed around in the Town Hall. Arthur Wormell will never be Poet Laureat. And Bag o' Nails will never, ever, *ever* be seen to smile.

Which brings me to the one person in the Straggling Town who has been worrying about the millennium. Ever since the arrival in our skies of the comet Hale Bopp last year, Bag o' Nails has been forecasting doom and disaster of Biblical proportions. First, the year's heavy rainfall convinced him of a need to enrol for a boat-building class at the local technical college. Next, he's been casting an anxious eye towards Heysham Power Station, convinced that the China Syndrome could become a reality before the century is out. Before he'll even venture out of doors these days he sends to the poultry dealers for a fresh undressed rabbit and spends the morning picking through the entrails at his kitchen table looking for bad omens. And the news that India and Pakistan are trying to outdo each other in destabilising the earth's crust with nuclear tests has put him in such a state that when he's not at the bar of the Poet and Peasant beating his breast and shouting 'Woe and alack!' he's trailing around town with a sandwich board bearing the slogans 'Repent' on the front, and at the back, naturally, 'The end is in sight!'

And an even more bizarre turn to his behaviour might have been noticed by anyone chancing to peep over his backyard wall recently. Bag o' Nails was spending an extraordinary amount of time in his bike shed. This might not seem so remarkable until you understand that he no longer had a bike to repair. He'd sold it, convinced, quite sensibly, that cycling on the public highway was as good for the human lungs as sniffing mustard gas. And the only things left in the shed were half-a-dozen tins of Jeyes Fluid and a broken trouser press. Closer inspection would have revealed that his visits to the shed were interrupted. After several minutes inside he would emerge wearing a long and very baggy gaberdine raincoat bulging somewhat in the lower regions. Looking more bent than ever at his stooping, world-weary shoulders and staggering slightly, he would cast an anxious glance about before disappearing out of the back gate and into the willow bushes on the spare ground opposite. Here, he would furtively open his mac and remove a large pump bag, which his mother had once made for him to take to school and still bore his embroidered initials, and empty a quantity of soil and stones from it. Then he would return to the bike shed before repeating the operation.

Admirers of the prisoner-of-war film, *The Wooden Horse*, will have rumbled what Bag o' Nails was up to. His bike shed was his wooden horse. It was not so much what was in it but what was under it which preoccupied him. Concealed from the watchful eyes of the world he was burrowing down beneath it like a busy termite, fashioning his very own safeguard against the millennium disaster. He was hollowing out a bunker where he might survive whatever Apocalypse Fate might fling at mankind on that fateful midnight.

Now I say that all this was going on concealed from the eyes of the world, but such a thing is not possible here in the Straggling Town. You can *think* something, just once, behind locked doors and with a pillow over your head, and someone will get to know what it is. Nosiness is elevated to an art form with us and I'm surprised they're not doing degree courses at the local college. It just so happened that the arch nosey Parker of all time lived next door to Bag o' Nails in Disraeli Street. The Red One. Yes, Red Eileen was his neighbour and it didn't take her long to spot that there was something going on in the bike shed. And when he'd finished removing those bags of soil and had begun carrying in there tins of luncheon meat and baked beans, Red Eileen was ready to announce to the whole world, from the red formica-topped table in the Cosy Cafe on the market that her neighbour had a secret bolt hole that was probably going to be used for some lewd purpose.

But she didn't.

The reason she didn't – and this will come as a shock to those of you who think her heart was made from anthracite – was that Red Eileen had a soft spot for Bag o' Nails.

Of course she never showed it in public. Her credibility as the greatest scourge of malekind since Queen Boadicea would have been lost. But there were moments, hidden moments, when she had cast her silken hook in his direction. The time she had pegged out a pair of saucy French knickers on the backyard line and hoisted them up with the clothes prop like a little flag of surrender. Or the occasion she had stood at her bedroom window when she knew he was out in the yard at night splitting slugs with a bread knife, and, leaving a tantalising chink in the curtains, stood in front of the bedside lamp in a see-through nightie. But all this had been in vain. Cloaked in his black cloud of misery and rarely looking up unless to ponder the chances of being struck by a falling meteorite, Bag o' Nails saw nothing of the amorous wiles of the red-haired siren from number 23.

Bag o' Nails' excavations were at a critical phase. Taking a leaf out of the book of the ancient pharaohs, he had devised a plan for sealing off his escape from this world. It wouldn't do if, come the dreadful catastrophe, others were to attempt to enter his refuge and plunder his supplies of spam and dandelion and burdock. So, once Doomsday arrived, the mouth of his shelter would transform into a giant hopper. The larger stones which he had unearthed during his excavations had been carefully stacked against the walls of the bike shed. Once safely inside his dug-out, he would pull a lever, the floorboards would tilt and the stones would come tumbling down and seal him safely in. (The problem of re-emerging was one he intended to deal with during his long sojourn with the moles and the worms ...)

It was late as Bag o' Nails was putting the crucial finishing touches to the lever. Red Eileen, having spent a pleasant evening with the girls drinking Cherry Bs after their spot-welding class, observed the activity in the shed from her boudoir. In a sudden impulse, driven by a mixture of curiosity and amorousness, she decided to go down and see for herself what he was up to. Throwing the diaphanous shift which in see-through turquoise went with the alluring nylon nightie, her magnificent bouffant released from the support of its scaffolding of pins and allowing her red tresses to fall upon her shoulders like fire spilling from the sides of an active volcano, she hurried down into next door's yard.

Bag o' Nails was below ground at the entrance to his bunker when the shed door was flung open. There in the threshold, the moonlight igniting her fiery tresses, the turquoise nightie billowing about her sturdy limbs like giant moth wings about two mighty candles, was a vision to strike terror into any male heart. Taking it to be the Angel of Death come to warn him of the imminence of the millennium catastrophe – Bag o' nails pulled the lever. Red Eileen could only watch as the object of her amorous desire disappeared in a cloud of stones and rubble like an ill-fated tower block. She had put the fear of death up many a man before, but never to such a dramatic effect.

When we finally dug him out he was prepared to defend himself to the last with his Great Uncle Albert's First World War bayonet. It took us a long time to persuade him we weren't after his supply of baked beans and that the Straggling Town was still standing. Only by bringing him a freshly pulled pint of Braithwaite's bitter from the Poet and Peasant was he convinced that he'd witnessed a false alarm. Nevertheless, every time he sees Red Eileen from now on he runs. But then, that's a normal enough male reaction.

Chapter Eighteen

'It's for you-ooh!'

*W*E'VE NEVER been ones for telephones here in the Straggling Town. We prefer eye-to-eye contact during our conversations and resent being rung up by double-glazing sales people during tea. And to stand in a huddle on the open market, with the wind flapping the canvas sides of the fruit and veg stall, might not seem a very comfortable place to talk about varicose veins or treacherous husbands, but it costs nowt. There isn't an invisible meter whirring away somewhere counting every sigh or 'She never!' I suppose – and this is something the telephone people with all their clever sales talk will never get past – we're a bit frightened of them. We still think that if a telephone rings it must be something important. Bag o' Nails won't answer a phone in case it's bad news. We just can't get it into our heads that you can interrupt someone from whatever they're doing just for a natter. Phones are for emergencies, in our book: things that won't wait. I once watched Arthur Wormwell answer a phone and he started whistling when he walked towards it. He always does that when he's trying to keep his courage up. He doesn't know I know that, but it's true. Arthur's very nervous about phones. He still believes they have operators and that people are listening in and writing down any unorthodox views they might hear.

And as for mobile phones, nobody has one of those apart from that pompous twerp Percy Smallcroft from the local paper. He reckons that the news he gets can't wait and must be phoned straight in. But we've never seen a story of his in the paper that wasn't ancient history. His mobile phone is the pathetic prop of a weak personality. It makes people like him seem important. For, however much phone companies may try to get rich by telling us that picking up a phone is as natural as drawing breath, see how self-conscious mobile phone-users are. 'Look at me,' they say, as they stand in the middle of the pavement or chuckle happily into the receiver aboard a crowded train or in a silly four-wheel drive, 'I'm such a big deal, people can't wait to speak to me and pass on important messages.' But we know they've asked people to ring them so that it looks good, and all they're really talking about is the cat's boil or whether or not they've to get mushy peas with the jumbo haddock and chips for tea.

So what a surprise when someone so natural and self-effacing as Arthur Wormwell, someone who knows that whatever he does it will never have any bearing on the great cosmic scheme of things, suddenly acquires a mobile phone. And no wonder he scowled, because it was worrying him to death.

'What's that you've got in your pocketses?' demanded Jimmy Capstick, observing the tell-tale rectangular bulge in Arthur's trouser pocket as he sat down at his bar stool at the Poet and Peasant Working Men's Club and his pants grew tight.

'Nothing,' snapped Arthur defensively.

'It's one of those thingy phones,' persisted Jimmy.

'Is not,' said Arthur, trying to cross his legs to conceal it.

'What is it then?' demanded Jimmy with the relentlessness of one of those creatures you sometimes see crossing the road like a ripple of rope and that can rip out a rabbit's throat in one bite.

'It's a book,' said Arthur desperately.

'It can't be a book, it's too small,' retorted Jimmy.

'It's a little Bible,' insisted Arthur.

'Pooh, a Bible? You? I thought you were a septic,' said Jimmy, who often gets words wrong.

'All right, then,' said Arthur miserably. 'It's a mobile phone. And I wish to God I'd not got it.'

And he took it out of his pocket and put it gingerly on the bar top as if it was an unexploded bomb.

We all waited for an explanation while Jack Lonsdale pulled him a pint.

Now Arthur Wormwell's Auntie Ethel had been a very odd customer. She was a leading light of the Nehemiah Spiritualist Church, a somewhat unprepossessing asbestos hut with a stove pipe chimney at the back of Mizpah Street and a Wednesday night meeting place for a small group of elderly Straggling Town matrons with an unshakable conviction that life as we know it will not end with the hollow ring of the gravedigger's shovel or the eerie final twitch of those velvet curtains at the crematorium. Convinced that nothing but a slender veil separated us from this world and the next, they had spent their evenings, bony hands united round a green baize card-table, in attempted conversation with those who had passed on. But last week, it had been Arthur's Auntie Ethel's turn to make the journey. After a somewhat unwise late supper of Gorgonzola cheese and silverskin onions, washed down with a bottle of milk stout, followed by a particularly unsettling late night horror film entitled 'They Came from Beyond the Grave', she had gone to put out the cat and fallen headlong down the unlit back-yard steps and into the Great Beyond.

Now Arthur had been Auntie Ethel's only surviving relative and to him had fallen the sad duty of sorting out her final affairs, not least the funeral arrangements. Only that afternoon, Arthur had stood at the grave-side in the Straggling Town cemetery with a cold wind blowing off Blackedge Reservoir and pinching the faces of the ladies from the Nehemiah Spiritualist Church who had assembled to say goodbye to one of their stoutest members.

Now I say 'Goodbye', but perhaps the expression I should be using is 'au revoir', which, as we all know, translates as 'I'll be seeing you.' For the good ladies of the Nehemiah Church were in no doubt that Ethel would be returning to them by next Wednesday night's meeting, if not before. And so was Ethel. So much so, that she had made arrangements of her own in case the normal channels of communication broke down.

At the time of the burial, the only person who knew about this was the undertaker, the slimy little Horace Fenwick of Horace Fenwick & Sons, Funeral Directors, 'Bereavement is our Business.' With a knowing smirk on his face, Horace stood there in his mourning coat and tails like a stunted penguin, supervising the lowering of Auntie Ethel's mortal remains into her, er, temporary resting place. Only when the short graveside ceremony was at an end and, as principal mourner, Arthur stepped into the first of the two 1956 Humber Hawks which comprised what Horace Fenwick liked to advertise in the *Straggling Town Examiner* as 'a modern fleet of limou-sines', did the undertaker reveal his little secret.

Now, I'm told that it's not unusual for the deceased to have all sorts of unusual requests about what they would like to have buried with them. Passionate devotees of the late, great Elvis Presley have been known to be buried with their entire Elvis LP collection. In this age of football fanaticism it is not uncommon for a supporter to want to be buried in full replica kit, with scarf, Thermos full of Bovril and rattle. In the case of our local team, who each season seem to flirt with disappearing into footballing oblivion themselves, the chances of the fan meeting up again with his heroes is not as crazy as it sounds. And, it appears that Auntie Ethel had her own special instructions about what was to be placed alongside her in her coffin. Horace Fenwick ran a small, podgy hand across his thin mouth as he tried to adjust a sarcastic smile.

'She was very insistent about it,' he told Arthur. 'Very.'

Arthur had to wait what seemed like an eternity for the revelation as the undertaker worked his way through the stubborn gears of the ancient limousine.

'You have to humour them. It's no good ignoring final demands,' he said, making it sound like something from the gas board. Arthur bit his lip while he waited. They were passing through the main street and caps were being raised by the old men on the seats outside the library. Arthur felt time freeze, as if it was he who was dead.

'She made me put a mobile phone inside with her, in case she wanted to get in touch,' announced Horace Fenwick chirpily.

So Auntie Ethel had been mad after all, thought Arthur at the news of this latest eccentricity.

'But that's not all,' said Horace Fenwick with a smirk. He loved saving the best bits for the last. It was the mark of a good undertaker.

'There's another one here for you, for when she finally rings through.' And he passed Arthur the small rectangular instrument.

With growing nervousness we gazed at it as it lay there on the bar at the Poet & Peasant Working Men's Club. Beer remained untouched.

'Is it possible?' asked Jimmy Capstick, his voice drier than ever.

'Who knows what lies beyond the grave,' boomed Bag o' Nails, and we wished he'd never spoken.

'But ... She couldn't see to dial inside a coffin,' said Jimmy Capstick, hanging on by his fingernails to the rational world; the cosy, comfortable world of the Straggling Town; the world of certainties: of Braithwaites Bitter at one pound ten pence a pint and a pie and pea supper on a Friday night; of being assured of a warm welcome on the market and not being able to get any sense out of anybody at the Town Hall. Our world. Warm and daft as a puppydog, but solid and reliable as paving flags and the houses in Balaclava Street. Not this. Not waiting for a phone call from the grave.

'She might not be in her coffin any more,' said Bag o' Nails, and Jimmy Capstick let out a whimpering sound like a child who sees the light go out at the top of the stairs and the shadows shuffle closer.

Then the phone rang.

People leapt back from the bar as if it had bitten them. Glasses toppled, beer swam. Six pairs of eyes gaped at the mobile phone. Grown men, some of whom had manned pillboxes against the cunning Hun during the war, quailed like fieldmice.

'It's for you,' whimpered Jimmy Capstick, burning to Arthur Wormwell.

Arthur's Adam's apple refused to swallow. His feet were welded to the spot. His eyes, behind his glasses, were two bowls of panicking fish. 'But ...' he tried, and failed.

'It's only your Auntie,' said Jack Lonsdale, who'd left his place behind the bar and had his coat on. For some reason his words failed to reassure.

Arthur Wormwell began inching towards the phone like a novice on a high wire. Time stood still again and we all savoured eternity. His hands shaking horribly, he reached for the receiver. His words took shape slowly, like water freezing over.

'Hello?'

The silence was so profound, we all heard the voice at the other end. It was halting and broken, fragmented words, searching for their real shape and meaning.

'-low, -low, -low. -gotten … grave. -orry. -o -orry.'

'Where are you?' gasped Arthur like a stricken thing. 'What is it like? What can you see? Tell us! Tell us!'

There was a long silence, then the line crackled. Then, suddenly, like a creature that has been caught in tangled undergrowth, the voice shook itself free.

'Fenwick here,' came a familiar sound. ''orace Fenwick, Funeral Directors, 'Bereavement is our Business'. Look here, I seem to have forgotten to put the phone in the grave with her after all. I'm sorry. Would you like us to dig her up again?'

'No,' came a chorus of voices. And, grown unusually thirsty from our experience, everyone hurried back to the bar.

Normality returned with the relieved sigh of Braithwaites bitter being eased out of the handpump into our glasses.

'What shall I do with this now?' asked Arthur, holding up the mobile phone. And we all took it in turns to jump upon it.

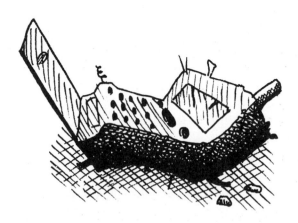

Chapter Nineteen

An Epiphany in Disraeli Street

A BREATHLESS CALM had settled over the Straggling Town. It was the time of year they call the halcyon days, around the winter solstice, when the wind that howls around the high moors and whistles down our narrow valley for most of the year, grows hushed. It happens every year without fail and must be magical. Nature holding its breath in awe before we all remember the nativity of that child they called The Prince of Peace.

Out over Widdop reservoir even the seagulls weren't their usual squabbling selves. They wheeled silently over the blackening waters, the last rays of the sinking sun catching fire in their feathers until they swirled and eddied like sparks from a bonfire. The surrounding moors crouched like enormous beasts, subdued, stretched out to sleep under the wide, wild sky whose light spilled over the rim of the world, pushed out by the gathering tide of darkness. But to show that light will always triumph over darkness, the stars began to stoke their own fires. Venus shone, steady as hope, and the lamps of the stars pricked slowly through the spreading canopy of gloom.

All this, of course, was ignored in the Straggling Town. You can't be gawping at the skies with Christmas just round the corner. Any kind of cosmic calm had been replaced by a frantic last-minute rush, nowhere more so than on the Open Market. The queue for turkeys at Fred Chadwick's butchers stretched as far as the tripe stall. Which didn't please Her-from-the-Tripe-Stall one bit. You see, she was doing rather poor business, and there's nothing more irksome than people queuing at your stall who are going to spend their money at someone else's. Her eyes bore the same cold glaze as the tripe itself, marooned in its enamel trays, stuck in that no-man's land between fish and fowl, along with other pale mysteries of the cow's insides like elder and chitterlings. 'Move on now, if you're not buying owt, and mek room for them as is,' she cried tetchily, prodding at a slice of bleached udder spitefully with her sharp fork until it shook wetly and a small boy who was passing with his mother tugged at her arm and shouted, 'Look at that jellyfish, mam!'

Fred Chadwick was hard to identify in his hanging garden of turkeys. Each bird was hung upside down from the roof, with a number on a brown label and a plastic cup round its neck to catch the drips of blood from its beak. And deep within this cavern of goosepimpled flesh was Fred, his face as red and livid as a turkey's wattles, or as a turkey's wattles once were before the butcher's knife slit its crop and the colour drained away with its life. His blood pressure was up like mercury in a heatwave. With a whole bough of mistletoe in his hat he was a Lord of Misrule let loose in a nunnery. Every female customer for whom he had harboured a steak-red passion the whole year long – and that went for any female from sixteen to eighty-five in the Straggling Town – he swooped upon from his forest of turkeys, grabbed with chumpy pink chipolata fingers and bestowed a kiss of such suction it nearly brought down the canvas awning over the market stall.

'Any more for stuffing?' he cried, wielding a truncheon of forcemeat like a drum majorette in a Whit procession. And his assistant, a lad of fifteen with pimples like smallpox, blushed to the hem of his oversized apron and hid his confusion behind a mountain of Paxo that reached to the roof.

In the back of his van, which served as a wet fish stall, Fleetwood Norman was as glum as a beached whale. Just why people had to boycott fish at Christmas, he'd never know. Wasn't the fish an early Christian symbol? We should be immersing ourselves in the stuff at Christmastide, he'd argued to his only customer, a little old lady who, taking him to be one of those born-again missionaries who sometimes set up camp in our market and want a donation, fled, leaving behind her bag of sprats unpaid for. Fleetwood's vision of tables groaning with buttered sprouts, golden roast potatoes and thick red cranberry sauce while Dad, in a paper cracker-hat, carved a lump of codfish, was too radical for the Straggling Town. It's hard enough trying to keep traditions alive with Gary Glitter blaring out of the speakers on the record stall instead of choirboys singing Noel, with kids queuing at Santa's cardboard grotto for laser pens to blind busdrivers instead of nuts and a tangerine, and more and more people looking forward to Christmas Day on the beach with a plate of paella in Tenerife. Tradition was sinking as slowly and remorselessly as the *Titanic* in all those videos everybody was buying.

We were discussing this very subject in the Poet and Peasant Working Men's Club where we'd put in an early appearance to sink a few pints of a special Christmas brew with which the brewery always marks the festive season. Known as Silent Night it packs sufficient of a punch to guarantee that the imbiber will not be disturbed by any activity at all within the

chimney flue during Christmas Eve. As members of the club's Public
Protection Committee, we would have been neglecting our duties had we
not undertaken a preview of the ale's properties to gauge how many pints
would be safe for our members to enjoy and still be in command of their
senses during the Queen's message to her subjects the following afternoon.

'By 'eck!' cried Arthur Wormwell, slapping his lips like a masseur working
on the belly of a sumo wrestler, 'I've not tasted better.'

The response was a contented sigh from the rest of the table as eyes
gazed dreamily at the world through amber-filled glasses and at a head as
tight and creamy as Jersey milk.

But the spell was soon broken. 'To absent friends,' said Jimmy Capstick,
raising his glass.

He was referring to Bag o' Nails. Our very own megalith of misery had
finally buckled under the cloud of pessimism that for as long as we had
known him had bent his broad shoulders and furrowed his brow. He had
announced that as far as he was concerned, Christmases were over. He
proposed to stay indoors and ignore the occasion until the last piece of
tinsel was stowed safely inside the Hoover bag and the plastic reindeers
had come down from the lamposts outside the town hall.

No amount of persuasion would convince him that even he would be
missed from our merry gatherings at the Poet and Peasant; that his
lugubrious presence was as much a part of our traditional enjoyment as a
thunderstorm on a Bank Holiday or an own goal down Turf Moor; that
life without downers was as dull as chips without vinegar; that real pleasure
needs a modicum of hardship to give it savour, and life in the Straggling
Town over Christmas just wouldn't be the same without our very own
pain-in-the-neck at our sides.

But Bag o' Nails was adamant. He'd had enough, he said. Enough silly
spending; of naked greed decked out in a red coat and a white beard. For
him there'd be no more listening to the cracked bells of drunken fellowship; of sprawling in a chair while the television moguls unwrapped their
tawdry Christmas treats. He was no longer prepared to gorge and sate
his appetites while the planet grew sick and three-quarters of the world
starved. Instead he'd sit it out until the whole grotesque pantomime was
over.

And with this Biblical condemnation of life as we know it, he drew the
two heavy bolts on the front door of 21 Disraeli Street, closed his curtains,
and pulling on a woollen Balaclava and his great uncle Albert's ginger raglan
overcoat, he prepared to pass the festive season at the kitchen table with
only a storm lantern for light and heat, a pound of Yorkshire tea and a

gross of pot noodles to sustain him, and the Harmsworth Encyclopaedia of Pestilence and Human Misery to keep him entertained.

Christmas Eve passed in the usual last minute scramble for belated presents and forgotten cards and enough supermarket bread to feed the five thousand without the aid of divine miracles. The weather continued to hold its breath. The sun set like a vast holly berry in the windless ocean of an azure sky. Starfire crackled out of the baffling infinitude of space. Nothing marred the sublime perfection of the end of another day in the four billion year history of the world. Well, nothing that the busy citizens of the Straggling Town had noticed. A more watchful eye might have seen, bubbling slowly out of the crimson eddies of the disappearing sun, a peculiar cloud. First it was crimson itself, but as it rose it was transformed into a glittering silver sphere. At a casual glance you may have thought it was the moon with all her imperfections ironed out, but insubstantial like silken gauze, and perfectly round, a wafer of light from some celestial communion table. Steadily and unnoticed it climbed the sky until it finally came to rest over the Straggling Town.

All night long the Pack o' Lies pub burst at the seams like a sack full of puppies. Beery bonhommie flowed by the barrel full. People got drunk, argued, and made up again. They shook your hand and forgot to let go for ten minutes. Mr Wang Lee's Chinese chippie bridged the gap between a long and liquid supper and tomorrow's turkey with polystyrene trays full of chips struggling to stay afloat in lava fields of curry gravy. Heads bowed at the New Age Bingo Parlour as it if was a prayer meeting. No one looked up. No one saw the strange and perfect cloud, fizzing inside its halo of silver light. And it had moved again, even closer, until it was hovering right over the rooftop of number 21 Disraeli Street.

Inside, Bag o' Nails had long been in bed. The steam from his hot, discontented breath had condensed on the ice-cold bedroom window and was making forests of frost. To keep warm he'd left on his Balaclava and piled his mother's old peg rug over the eiderdown. It smelt of coal and old footprints and the dog he'd once had but had died. Bag o' Nails was not asleep. His eyes were tightly shut to squeeze out the bad world and his gums were clamped grimly together. An old wooden clock ticked ominously, growling before every chime, and his false teeth grinned vacantly from the bedside table.

It wasn't just the sound of late-night revellers tumbling down the backstreets like noisy tin cans that was keeping him awake. A heavy chain of misery hung about his heart. Nothing seemed to lighten it these days. Age had long dissolved all the hope of youth and life seemed to be nothing

but a comfortless path towards sickness and death. A conviction that humanity was lost in a senseless world of selfish gratification poisoned whatever happiness was left to him. And the truth of his voluntary exile from the rest of us lay in the fact that the thought of Christmas, with all its memories of the past, of lost innocence and simple pleasures, was now too painful for him to contemplate. He'd rather shut it out forever.

'What's the point?' he cried miserably from underneath the dusty peg rug.

And suddenly, with a crack like gunshot, the hardboard screen which covered the old bedroom fireplace flew into the hearth in a shower of soot. A fizzing beam of silver light burst down the chimney, hit the floor and jagged up onto the bedroom wall where it danced like starfire.

Bag o' Nails sat bolt upright in bed shaking from his gums to his bedsocks. Even his false teeth on the bedside table began to chatter.

Slowly, the swirling plasma of light began to take on recognisable shapes. First there were words.

'Hello, old misery guts,' said the shining wall.

Bag o' Nails' eyes grew round as milk tokens.

'So nothing's worth it anymore?' went on the wall. And then, 'Well maybe you'd better take a look at this.'

And suddenly he was looking right inside the house of Hilda-the-Ton. He knew it was hers because he'd once gone in to help get a pigeon out of her attic. There she was on the landing in a nightie like a marquee, tip-toeing so daintily to make sure the loose floorboards didn't creak. She was taking a stocking with a train set, some colouring books and a newly knitted cardigan into her Colin's room. Colin was grown up, except for his mind, and Hilda had to do everything for him. And even though she'd had a long day and her varicose veins were playing up, she'd waited up till after one and Colin was settled to be Father Christmas, like she'd done every year since he was a baby, so that when he woke up bright and early he'd find his presents there at the bottom of the bed.

Then the scene changed and it was Red Eileen he saw this time. At least, he thought it was Eileen. He'd never seen her like this before. She'd let down her huge bouffant and her red locks spilled down as far as her waist. And she'd taken off that ugly red smear of lipstick that made her look so frightening when she was out. Now she looked much softer, and if you closed your eyes a bit and ignored those lines that life and three broken marriages had etched into her face, she was quite pretty. She was sitting at the bedside of an old man and feeding him broth, dabbing his chin with a cloth where he dribbled and making soft encouraging sounds. It was her Dad who'd been bed-ridden for fourteen years and needed looking after day and night, and of whom she vowed, 'They'll never put him in a home. Not over my dead body!'

And then a third domestic scene, one that took Bag o' Nails' breath clean away. It was Jurassic Jeff, football hooligan and roaring boy, who drank sixteen pints of lager as an aperitif and was responsible for more broken noses than the entire front row of the Wigan rugby scrum. And there, in those giant arms, snuggling amongst the tattoos of serpents, dragons and dripping daggers, a tiny pink bundle of baby, Jurassic Junior. And his dad is giving him his middle of the night feed from a titty bottle, and has stayed sober as a priest on Christmas Eve to do it!

'The big things in the world might be a mess,' spoke the light, 'but it's the little things that folk go on doing that give us hope. And there's all this as well. Have you forgotten?'

And the scene changed to outdoors. It was the wood on Warcock Hill where they'd played as children: building dens in the secret heart of the rhododendron thickets, damming the stream below the waterfall and paddling, hunting for the hidden nests of wrens under the overhanging roots of the beech trees. Now it was all awash with moonlight, running like molten solder across the fellside; waking the shadows, burning the bare branches of the trees until they were etched black against the sky like the tracery of some wild cathedral. And the stars beyond, proud in their frigid majesty: the glittering Pleiades, Cassiopeia like a giant bird and Orion striding forever acros the limitless universe. And he saw a fox stealthily nosing through the fallen leaves of Autumn that were still golden, and an owl swoop from his perch in the Scot's pine for something only owls can see. And, because it was magic, he heard a robin piping a sweet song, awake in the moonlight.

'It's all still here,' spoke the light, and Bag o' Nails stretched out his hand to write his name upon this earthly paradise.

Next morning, people passing, hurrying to take their presents to friends and neighbours, were amazed to see that Bag o' Nails' curtains were drawn back. A holly wreath had appeared on his front door and through the fanlight above – it was hard to see because the glass was a bit dirty – they swore they could make out some Christmas trimmings. And around lunchtime, when we all pop into the Poet and Peasant to oil the gastric juices before Christmas dinner, who should we find, long nose dipped into a pint of Silent Night, but our own Christmas exile, Bag o' Nails.

'Drinks are on me,' he cried, causing Jimmy Capstick to come close to a heart attack.

And to show that miracles, like sneezes, always come in pairs, Bag o' Nails smiled.

'Happy Christmas,' he cried. 'And many more of 'em.'

Chapter Twenty

The Night of the Pigs

*I*T IS ONLY STRANGERS to the Straggling Town who are surprised to learn that the members of the Poet and Peasant Working Men's Club share their premises with a herd of pigs. To those of us who live here it seems entirely natural that the rambling outbuildings should be put to good use, and what better than the nurture of the raw material for that most delicious of local delicacies, the pork pie? And to any outsider fortunate enough to be invited into the cosy bar on a cold November evening to sit shoulder to shoulder with us, savouring the delights of a pint of Old Rapture and basking in the warmth of wit and fellowship for which our club is renowned, the thought of happy, wallowing pigs would never be far from his mind.

But considerations like this apart, both pigs and men are content to lead their separate lives. That was until the extraordinary events of a certain Friday night which has rightly gone down in local folklore as The Night of the Pigs.

The catalyst for the drama, as is so often the case with incidents at the Poet and Peasant, was beer. Not just any old beer, and none of your chemically spiked lagers which every night of the week, in any part of the country, can send young men on the rampage. No, this was the product of a small, somewhat secretive brewery over the hill in darkest Yorkshire, the home of Old Rapture, and on this occasion, a barrel so sublime that had it been wine it would have had vintage stamped all over it and the cogniscenti clawing at each other's throats to get hold of it.

'By gum, this is nectar,' cried Arthur Wormwell, smacking his lips like a dray horse. Murmurs of agreement muffled by froth came from all around.

'I wonder what their secret is?' mused Fred Chadwick the butcher, a restless seeker after perfection, as his own pork pies and sausages testified.

'Ours not to reason why, Ours but to drink it dry,' said I, knowing where my duty lay.

'Aye,' brooded Bag o' Nails, the only man amongst us for whom drink never bred content, only deeper melancholy. 'It'll not last.'

His words broke the spell, for at that moment the beer pump began making that dry sucking sound that brought only bubbles to the glass that was being refilled and universal despair to our hearts.

'Sorry, lads,' said Jack Lonsdale the steward, 'It's dead.'

Our stay in heaven was cut short. The grey limbo of abstinence beckoned.

'Can't you put another one on?' pleaded Jimmy Capstick, a small man with a throat like a furnace.

'Nay, lads,' shook the steward, looking at his watch. 'It's nearly twelve. We need to shut. Anyway, I've not got another one ready. You've gone through that at a fair rate of knots.'

'Like pigs at cherries,' sighed Arthur, and if we'd not been so preoccupied with our own misery we might have heard a grunt of fellow feeling from the sty next door. Reluctantly we turned to the door, to head for our beds and dreams of endless fountains of Old Rapture in a land where time stands still.

Meanwhile, a single act of carelessness was about to set in motion the terrible events that were to shatter the peaceful slumber of so many.

Just as pearls must be worn for their real beauty to be awakened, or so I'm told, so Old Rapture must be nurtured to bring out its unearthly qualities. No one knew this better than Jack Lonsdale, and it earned him undying respect in all our hearts. Where a lesser man who had consumed the same amount as he had that night would have gone straight to bed to sleep it off, Jack was ever mindful of his duties as custodian of the great elixir. If the next barrel was to be as good as the last, certain rituals must be observed. Swaying like a tug in an Atlantic swell, he made his way to the cellar. This was a small room situated between the bar and our animal neighbours next door. Here he disconnected the defunct barrel and fixed the line to a water supply used to flush out any sediment that might be lurking in the system ready to adulterate the fresh barrel. This was already vented and waiting on the still in readiness for tomorrow night's eager supplicants. However, as he bent to his work, a sudden rush of alcohol-replete blood to his brain caused a moment's giddiness, and as he lurched to regain his balance he stuck out an arm. This was enough to dislodge one of the wedges underneath the new barrel. But, as become the demons which possess all inanimate objects – even things as noble as barrels of Old Rapture – the full effects of the accidental displacement were not immediate. Only after Jack had closed the cellar door did the barrel lurch to one side and with an impish chuckle the sublime fluid trickled away to the floor, untasted and unappreciated.

Well, not quite. By some quirk of the club's ancient plumbing system, the drainage channel out into the stone floor of the cellar was in direct communication with a similar conduit next door. And this in turn led into a large stone trough used by the pigs. The animals couldn't believe their luck. Suddenly, into their midnight prison, this dark desert of the senses, comes a merry gurgling, and with it the most beautiful and irresistible smell. Something they've hankered after for so long. Something that comes from next door and makes men laugh aloud and shout. And now, like an answered prayer, it's on its way to meet them, whispering and singing in the dark. And filling their trough!

Six large pigs, blinking the sleep and disbelief out of their eyes, tip-toe to the trough. Six snouts savour the heavenly aroma. And then with a mad lunge the heads are in and they're sucking away for all their weight in bacon. And in no time at all, eighteen gallons of strong beer have disappeared into their bellies.

The effects of this alcoholic bonanza on the pigs were not dissimilar to what happens to humans. Like hot-blooded youngsters who have drunk themselves silly at the pub, they first set to amongst one another. They squabbled and squealed, nudged and nipped, spoiling for bother without really knowing why. Quiet years of domesticity dissolve as they are back in the forest, tusked and terrifying monsters ready to revel in their new found brutishness. It was a good job Jack Lonsdale had locked up and gone home, otherwise he could have been excused for thinking his club had been transformed into Jurassic Park. But when they tired of trying to gore one another, bite each other's ears off and taste lumps from each other's sides without the benefit of salt curing, they turned to wreaking havoc on the premises. This was the mindless vandalism phase of drunkenness. At first they threw themselves at the party wall from which the irresistible liquor had arrived, perhaps thinking there was more to be had if only they could dislodge the stonework. But finding that the pain even managed to penetrate their thick rind they soon gave up and concentrated on the wooden door. Being half-rotten and belonging to the local farming school of practice which decrees that nothing be replaced until it has disintegrated, the door offered very little resistance. But it was when the pigs found themselves outside that the trouble really began.

There was a full moon, and the pigs had never seen the moon before. It was not a bit like normal daylight where you had to screw up your pale eyelashes when you looked up into the sky. You could stare at this midnight sun and it stared back. Wistful, strange and sympathetic, it seemed to be saying, 'It's night now and you are safe with me. Men are not about, so why not enjoy yourselves?' And the dark line of the surrounding hills crouched closer and said, 'Yes, go on, we can keep it secret.' And the flitting, feral shadows crowded eagerly around and whispered, 'Yes. Go on. Let rip!'

And so the pigs let rip.

Like all good drunkards their first priority was more drink. Snouts to the earth, pale bottoms raised to the moonlight they pushed forward with the remorselessness of a rugby scrum. They ploughed straight into the yard at the back of The Pack o' Lies pub where their wonderful noses had detected the delectable smell coming from a pile of empties stacked against the cellar wall. They hit them like lard exocets, scattering crates and aluminium barrels in a din that sounded like a steel band in a motorway pile-up. Bag o' Nails, whose house overlooked the yard, woke from that first confused trough of sleep, and hearing the racket, groped under the bed for his copy of Protect and Survive. The landlord of the pub staggered downstairs and let out the dogs. The two giant Alsatians took one look at the pale, seething glanks of bacon and fled into the hills and weren't seen again for the best part of a week. Finding nothing to eat and soon tiring of crunching up empty bottles of Babycham, their fuddled brains turned to thoughts of food. A different barrel, with fluted sides and a lid, smelling promisingly of kipper skins, was attacked next. In no time, four dustbins were being rolled around the yard releasing an assortment of tit-bits, not least the remains of a garlic casserole whose after effects had proved too volatile for human consumption. It wasn't long before the beasts were rampaging the full length of Balaclava Street, upending every dustbin in sight in their quest for more supper. Telephone calls jammed the police switchboard with reports varying from an escaped hippo to the Gaderene swine on the loose. But since the local police station was unmanned out of office hours – which we all know is when all crime takes place – the calls had to be put through to headquarters twelve miles away, which gave the pigs plenty of time to wreak further mayhem. But then, something happened which had a sudden sobering effect on the animals.

When the pigs emerged onto the main street they were confronted with a smell entirely beyond their gastronomic spectrum. Yet it was so appealing it set their snouts drooling and their hearts racing with joy. The Chinese chippy was still open. The proprietor, Mr Wong, was hanging on to the bitter end in the hope that someone would be drunk enough to purchase the soggy apology for fish and chips that had been stewing away above the friers for over an hour. But he wasn't expecting the kind of customer he got. He looked up to find six pairs of trotters lined up on the counter and six pigs' heads fetchingly adorned with sprout leaves and potato peelings gazing over at him expectantly.

Now even in his short stay in the Straggling Town Mr Wong had grown used to dealing with some fairly unsavoury late-night customers. Every week-end he came face to face with bloodshot eyes and truculent jaws. He'd even learnt to translate the belligerent grunts that came his way on a wave of stale beer and send them off with their suppers without too much blood being spilt. But these were human customers – though some might argue the point. What faced him now was definitely not. And to leave him in no doubt, one of the pigs, clearly the ringleader to judge from the fact that it was the only one whose ears didn't look as if they'd been chewed, suddenly thrust its snout through the glass shelf, grabbed a battered cod and had it down its throat in the time it takes a butcher to shout 'Danish!' The rest followed suit and Mr Wong found himself in a position he'd never been in since taking over the business, with nothing at all left over.

He should have been pleased but instead he was furious. Raising a meat cleaver concealed behind the bar should he ever receive a visit from members of the Triad, he leapt around the counter to take payment for his fish in flesh. The pigs, sensible of something prophetic about the cleaver, made off into the night but not before the ringleader had swallowed a bottle of vinegar to go with his fish and chips. They got as far as the window of Fred Chadwick's butcher's shop when they were stopped in their tracks by a sight guaranteed to freeze even their smouldering corpuscles.

Hanging from a hook in the ceiling, eyes staring in mute appeal from between prone and polished trotters, was one of their brothers.

To a pig their stomachs lurched, and for the first time in their lives they lost their appetites. Cruelty they had known. Hadn't they in their infant years been snatched prematurely from that warm mountain of milk they'd never learnt to call their mother? How many times had they felt the steel capped boot of the farmer? But this was nothing compared to the cruelty they were now witnessing. Something must be done at once. Their brother must be rescued.

The ringleader launched his 220 pounds of quivering and indignant pork flesh at the plate glass window. But the crash, though enough to wake the dead failed to rouse Fred Chadwick from his torpor. He was deep in a dream of taking the Prix d'Honor in France's major black pudding festival. French mademoiselles clad in nothing but strings of his own shining puddings wriggled about him. But down below in the shop events were taking a much nastier turn. Attempting to dislodge his suspended brother, the ringleader pig suddenly observed that instead of a healthily replete stomach like his own, he bore the most frightful gash from chin to hind quarters from which the insides had been removed like peas from a pod.

Now, to a pig the loss of its stomach is the most unimaginable privation. His stomach is the very engine-room of his being, the prime-mover of his existence. A pig exists solely to satiate that organ. Without it he is nothing but pork scratchings. The ringleader let out a terrible keening cry of loss and rage unheard of since the great boar hunts of yore. The other pigs rushed to his side to stare in horror at their mutilated brother. Outrage gave birth to a lust for revenge.

Following their noses – for the smell of stale Old Rapture still hung about the staircase – they headed for the bedroom. Heaving flanks made matchwood of the banisters as they ploughed their way upstairs. Mrs Chadwick might have been expected to be awakened by the din but she was severely deaf and her only means of hearing lay at her bedside disconnected. It was only when the animals barged their way into the bedroom like a lynchmob, dislodging a large mahogany wardrobe in the process, that the noise of it crashing to the floor finally penetrated the silent chambers of Elsie Chadwick's ears. She awoke to find a living hell at her bedside. Surrounding her, ears pricked like horns, small eyes burning with vengeance, were six snorting and slavering demons with the vern stench of the eternal pit hanging over them. With a piercing scream she swooned back onto her pillow unconscious.

The cry of his helpmate, she who had plucked turkeys and stuffed forcemeat at his side, stirred Fred Chadwick from his dreams. His glossy puddings, and the equally glossy but lillywhite orbs of the playful made-moiselles they adorned, were rudely replaced by every butcher's nightmare. The spirits of those beasts whose blood lay on his hands had returned to torment him. What had been so many pounds of belly-pork, so many stand pies, was now a swinish Hydra come to exact revenge. He placed both hands over his eyes praying the ghastly apparition would depart.

But the pigs' rage gave way to puzzlement and then to pity. What sort of a place was this? Their brother had had his stomach removed, but these humans, whom they'd taken to be responsible, had suffered an equally shocking fate. Someone had removed their bodies. Heads only had stared back at them from the pink Paisley duvet. You can't expect pigs who have never seen human beings in bed before with the bedclothes pulled up to their chins to work out that this was what we did every night, not after three gallons of strong beer each. In fact, what with all the exercise and excitement of the night, the Old Rapture was beginning to have the effect it had on all sublunary creatures whose greed overcomes their discretion. As if to an invisible signal they suddenly all slumped down and fell into a fathomless sleep, punctuated only by the sound of snores and the frequent and noisy emission of gases from the volatile garlic casserole.

And so they slept on. Long after Fred Chadwick and his wife had been rescued in the morning. Long after the regulars at the Poet and Peasant had met again the following evening to weep over the loss of so much Old Rapture. In fact, they slept for four days. Only then could they be removed from the bedroom and restored to their normal premises, rather bad-tempered and red-eyed with fur quite visible on their normally pink tongues. Fred Chadwick and his wife were not so lucky. They were unable to return home. Despite the use of high pressure hoses and whole carboys of disinfectant, their bedroom was pronounced unfit for human habitation and they had to move. Fred now runs a vegetarian food stall on the open market and the poor man has not touched a drop of Old Rapture since. Nor have the pigs, though if we could reach into their minds we would find that they dream about it.

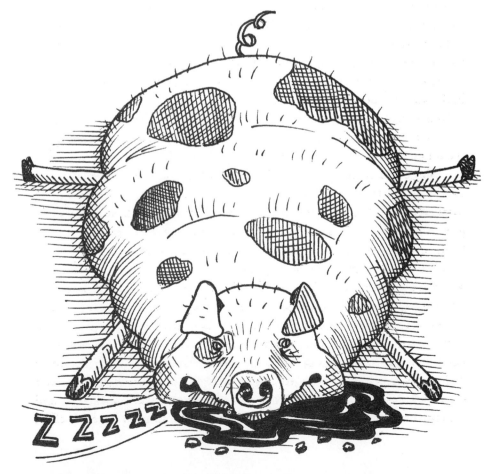

ZZZZZ

Chapter Twenty-One

Indian Spring

Spring was having trouble springing this year in the Straggling Town.
'Just look at this,' lamented Bag o' Nails, stamping a size twelve gardening boot onto the earth and releasing a cloud of dust. You might be forgiven for thinking the dust had come from Bag o' Nails' boots, they were so ancient. They'd been issued to him by the Home Guard along with a gas-mask and tin helmet, all of which he'd seen fit to keep despite the end of hostilities. 'You never know when they might be needed again,' he would say, scowling at the sky whenever the drone of an aircraft was to be heard.

It had been the driest winter anyone could remember and the showers of April, whose job it was to unlock the glories of the season, had resolutely refused to appear. The only thing that the weather had unlocked was the dark vault of pessimism that was Bag o' Nails' mind.

He pointed a gnarled finger at a row of stubborn shallots.

'They'd stand more chance in the Kalahari desert,' he moaned, before going on to forecast a gardening year plagued with drought of such Biblical proportions that the best we could do would be to sit cross-legged in the dust and wait for the Red Cross to airlift our vegetables in by Hercules.

But mercifully not everyone shared Bag o' Nails' gloomy outlook. It was the first Sunday of the year when the Allotment Society opened the hut at the bottom of the gardens and the members turned up to renew their subscriptions and buy the fertilizers and things they'd need for the next months. From the shadowy interior arose the smell of bonemeal and hydrated lime, and there, among the bamboo canes and stacks of Irish moss peat, was Ernest Fothergill dressed in a brown overall he'd kept from his days at the Co-op grocers, with an indelible pencil stuck behind his ear. Stooping over a bench like some ancient alchemist, he weighed out the bags of potash and sulphate of ammonia, all the rich fusion of ingredients to stir dull clay into colourful life, the magic that would make cabbages swell like footballs and chrysanthemums explode into giant sunbursts. And the rest of us watched like hawks, silently noting what everyone else was buying, hoping for a clue to their success at last year's Autumn show.

'What do you use that for?' asked Arthur casually.

'Them as asks no questions gets told no lies,' replied old Jack Robinson, and with a horny finger and thumb which had nipped more wireworms than Jack Frost nips late dahlias, he handed over his money and disappeared into the sanctuary of his own shed to mix up a potting compost potent enough to coax magnolias out of Accrington bricks.

Rain or no rain, for most of us it was a time of renewal of hope. Forgotten were the failures of last year: spinach that ran to seed faster than George Best, greenfly as voracious as locusts. And for Arthur and me, the pleasure of breaking the long winter siege was sweetened by nostalgia. Our dads had also had allotments here, and as lads, when we'd succeeded in escaping from the purgatory of being made to weed the empty strawberry beds, we'd run wild in the neighbouring woods, crawling through the tall grass of the long meadow playing Indians, and damming the beck until we'd made a swimming pool. Ah, if only time's stream was so easy to stem!

'What's old misery guts up to, then?'

A voice that could deadhead a begonia at fifty yards struck up from the back of the queue. A flash of red wellies and a matching raincoat announced the presence of Red Eileen like a distress flare. Her bright henna bouffant bristled aggressively. She'd been watching the antics of Bag o' Nails with a sardonic leer on her crimson lips. She was the sort of woman who could put chastity in the mind of men like Oliver Reed, and she was here to stock up on weedkiller and slug pellets.

Bag o' Nails was going through a long list of environmental outrages that he thought were responsible for our climatic changes, and all with nightmarish consequences. He was a barometer of impending disasters. It's how he got his name. You'd be driving along in the car with him and he'd spot an innocent paperbag in the road. 'Look out!' he'd shout, trying to grab the wheel. 'It might be a bag of nails!'

BAROMETER OF IMPENDING DISASTER

400 —
360 —
300 —
250 —
200 —
150 —
100 —
50 —
0 —

DOOM, DOOM, I say, DOOOM!

4 Horsemen of the Apocalypse!

'Old Rapture' recipe lost!

Red Eileen - Proposes marriage

Nuclear Holocaust

Ozone Depletion

Greenhouse Effect

Lost lucky Horseshoe

Slugs eat Cabbages

'You're right, man. The earth is dying.'

This perky contribution had come from a gaunt figure clad in an East German army greatcoat wearing a tea-cosy with two greasy pigtails emerging from the holes where the spout and handle were meant to go. He was one of our resident hippies. Distant galaxies could be plainly observed in his eyes, and he and his friends had been responsible for introducing some of the more exotic species of plant onto the allotments which certain dogs have been trained to sniff out. But nothing was said. We're very tolerant of eccentricities in the Straggling Town, otherwise where would the rest of us be?

Woodstock – for his mother had named him after the place of his conception – then announced that he had a friend who was a Red Indian, and he'd be quite happy, for a glass or two of Scrumpy Jack, to come over and do a rain dance.

Nobody had heard of any Indian reservations in the vicinity of the Straggling Town, and when we were told he was from Oldham the news was greeted with the sort of scepticism reserved for claims of a two pound gooseberry.

But as usual, our curiosity got the better of us and the turn out that evening on Woodstock's allotment was quite impressive.

It isn't often we tend to be on the allotments after dark. The last time was when there was a bent greengrocer on the loose who was digging up our potatoes and selling them on the Open Market. But being there tonight got us strangely excited. It was a bit like being kids again with candles in jamjars, huddled in our den on the railway embankment telling stories about the headless horseman of Wycoller. And when Woodstock lit a fire and our shadows started to flit and dance and merge with the larger shadow that was the night beyond, we all instinctively moved closer together as men and women down the ages always have when they felt the primal fear of darkness.

One person totally without fear was Red Eileen. Her red beehive hairdo flashed in the firelight like a bronze helmet. She'd brought her friend, Hilda-the-Ton, her whom no tape measure could encompass. Hilda was under the impression that she had been invited to a seance and had brought with her the false teeth of her late husband in the hope of tempting him back.

'Where is he, then?' demanded Eileen. 'This Big Chief Sitting Bull.'

The Indian, real name Wayne Grimshaw but adopted title Passing Grass, was at that moment in Woodstock's shed living up to his title and handing round the pipe of peace in the shape of a large roll-up. Only after several deep lungfulls was he able to make the mental journey from the corporation allotments in the Straggling Town to the foothills of Dakota.

When he finally emerged he looked very impressive in his flowing feathered headdress. Slashes of red warpaint adorned his face, reminiscent of the livid lipstick worn by Red Eileen and marketed under the name of Wilful Passion.

But the most sensational part of the show was yet to come. Unseen by the rest of us Woodstock had taken up a position in the shadows beyond the firelight. Seated on a pile of old Brussels sprouts stalks he clutched a geniune Indian deerskin drum, handcrafted in Hebden Bridge. As he began to strike it, a strange raw pulse unfurled from the darkness. It could have been the pulse of the earth itself, muffled as if Nature were still trapped in the grip of winter or life itself stifled by the arid season. And it touched a chord in all of us, echoing to the rhythm of the blood, and an irresistible urge to dance overtook us. Passing Grass was already dancing, beating a rhythmical tattoo on the earth with his feet, shaking his arms as if playing some invisible maracas; and wailing, a strange keening reproach at the plight of the sick earth which made the hair rise on our necks.

Soon we were all joining in. Hilda-the-Ton, her skirts billowing round her knees like some ceremonial elephant. Eileen, a terrifying warrior queen bathed in enemy blood. Arthur shuffling self-consciously because he'd never recovered from the trauma of being made to attend ballroom dancing classes at school. Bag o' Nails, pale and doleful like the Grim Reaper leading the dance of death. Even Puffing Billy Ridehalgh joined in, sixty full-strength cigarettes a day for the last forty years, his wheezing could be heard half a mile away.

Suddenly, at a signal from Passing Grass we all stopped.

'A sacrifice,' he cried. 'We need a sacrifice.'

Eileen's lips curled like a blood-stained sickle and Hilda got out the false teeth.

'It's got to be something of the earth,' said the Oldham Indian. 'Something the earth will recognise.'

Arthur disappeared into one of the sheds and emerged with a dark bundle.

'Onto the fire,' instructed Passing Grass.

It was too late by the time Bag o' Nails noticed. His boots were already beginning to burn.

That night the heavens opened and it rained for a week. And the next day, amid loud lamentations of financial ruin, Bag o' Nails went out and bought a new pair of boots. It was the dawn of a new spring in the Straggling Town.

Chapter Twenty-Two

An Incident at Balaclava

*T*HERE was a special buzz of excitement about the Market Hall this morning. It was like we used to get on the eve of a Wakes Week holiday when all the mills would shut, the looms clatter to a halt and the great steam engines stop like a panting beast lying down to sleep. Then there was the scarcely imagined luxury of a week to yourself. All the rumbustious fun of Blackpool if you could afford it, or if not, a quiet mooch about the hills and valleys of the Straggling Town with a picnic of a few butties and a bottle of water. Simple pleasures, easy to sneer at in an age of jets and package holidays to Spain and Disneyworld, but all the sweeter then when hard work ruled and fun was kept under lock and key for most weeks of the year.

Nowhere was the sense of expectation greater than at the Cosy Cafe. There, at a table in the middle that others could sit at at their peril, were the Straggling Town's answer to the Three Fates, in whose hands the thread of every reputation hung. Among the crusty necked bottles of brown sauce sat Red Eileen, Hilda-the-Ton and Her-from-Next-Door. Character assassination reached the same level of art as poisoning under the dreaded Borgias. Drinking tea as brown as ox-tail soup, and often as thick, and eating buttered Eccles cakes, nothing escaped their vinegar gaze. But today there was something less conspiratorial and much more self-important about them. Red Eileen was throwing back her henna bouffant like a triumphal cockerel.

'I should imagine His Royal Highness will want to speak to me,' she crowed, loud enough for the whole market to hear.

'You'll have to curtsy if he does,' said Hilda, looking rather worried at the prospect of a manoeuvre her own relentless corsetry would render impossible.

Eileen frowned. This was a consideration she'd overlooked. She would bow to no man, even if he was heir to the throne of England.

Her-from-Next-Door, a dry little woman with a voice that whined like a slipped fan-belt, chuckled mischievously. 'He's looking for a wife who can behave herself,' she said.

Eileen ignored her and settled herself into her seat with regal dignity. 'Mr Perry is particularly anxious that I should be there weaving on the day.'

Austin Perry, you will remember, was our new Director of Tourism. The product of some leafy campus of the Home Counties where the bogus sciences of management and marketing have replaced the patient arts of scholarship, he was a master of the oily skills of public relations. He was determined to beat a quick path to Chief Executive Officer by reviving the glories of our textile past. King Cotton was to be exhumed and his mummified remains put on show for tourists from far and wide. He had already opened a heritage trail along the Leeds and Liverpool Canal, renowned for its dead dogs and floating supermarket trolleys, and his latest triumph had been to restore the Balaclava Cotton Mill and its old steam engine. But Austin Perry's real scoop was to persuade the Prince of Wales to come to the official opening. Long live the silken tongue and oily palm!

As Red Eileen debated whether or not to forgo her customary red apparel for something purple for the great occasion, the visit was also the subject of conversation in the bar of the Pack o' Lies. Here, Percy Smallcroft of the *Straggling Town Examiner* was planning the coverage. We were discussing the last time royalty graced our humble doorstep. Arthur remembered it well. His uncle, he informed us, had worked for the corporation in those days and helped to erect no fewer than five toilets on the royal route, which no one reckoned could have been a distance of more than one mile.

'It's what they eat,' opined Jimmy Capstick. 'All that rich food.'

Percy Smallcroft tried to steer the conversation back onto more dignified lines. He wanted some background information on the mill engine and its operator, Walton Grinrod, who had been brought out of mothballs to supervise its restoration. Walton puffed away at his pipe, stubbornly adrift in a world of valves and sprockets.

'But isn't this steam engine too old?' argued Percy. 'It can't be very reliable after all these years.'

This was a fatal mistake to be made with Walton. As far as the old engineer was concerned it was an axiom of life that everything that appeared after 1945 was no good. This not only went for machinery but also newspaper reporters. As far as he was concerned society had come off the rails after the war and the only way to put it back was to return to a golden age when everyone worked with their hands making things to sell to a grateful world held in awe by our Empire, fleet of battleships and policemen not afraid to cuff boys round the earhole to stamp out wrongdoing.

The day of the royal visit dawned. It was raining heavily. Austin Perry, having taken a course in positive thinking, insisted that this could only be a good thing because the damp conditions had brought textiles here in the first place. This desire for authenticity had extended as far as to position a small group of local schoolchildren dressed in shawls and bonnets waving damp flags outside the mill to greet the royal motorcade. He was frankly disappointed that they all looked so plump and healthy and not a single case of rickets or consumption could be found anywhere in the Borough, though an outbreak of influenza did occur later because the royal visit was an hour behind schedule. It was a very low key affair compared to the last one forty years ago, a tribute to the success of the modern media to demystify the royal family, to say nothing of the ability of its younger members to shoot themselves, and their spouses, in the foot. One single pennanted limousine brought the prince. But what the visitor may have lacked in ostentation was made up for in abundance by the local reception committee. The mayor, Councillor Horace Slack, positively groaned under the weight of his civic regalia, wearing enough gold and jewellery round his neck to settle the national debt of Namibia. A covey of preening councillors and civic trust worthies stood by while the unctuous Austin Perry slid between them like graphite making the introductions. It was this dog's day and nothing was going to mar it and stand in his way of a knighthood. He smiled serenely at everyone, including the rather ugly security men who at that moment were looking suspiciously at Arthur at the back wearing his Michael Foot donkey jacket.

But the unexpected is often an uninvited guest at dos in the Straggling Town. So it was quite unexpected that Red Eileen, wearing a black shawl and clogs, with not a hint of purple, should curtsy so low when she was introduced to His Highness that she almost struck her head on the flagged floor. And it was entirely unexpected that the so-solid, sound-as-steel Walton Grinrod should so go to pieces under the gaze of His Royal Highness, and his mind so start to swim with visions of our country's antique greatness, that he should fail to notice that he'd left his cleaning rag on his beloved engine's governor rope. And that it had disconnected the drive, so, thinking the engine had stopped, the governor opened up the valves, and sent the giant flywheel hurtling round at such a speed that not even the sixty tons of cast iron of which it was made could withstand the frightful forces let loose. And by the time Walton did notice, all was lost.

And so would our respected prince have been, had not Arthur grabbed him by the lapels of his double-breasted Savile Row suit and dragged him away down the fire escape to safety. Nor was it to be expected that for his pains Arthur, instead of being decorated for his heroism, should be pounced upon by the security men and driven off at high speed to be interrogated by the anti-terrorist squad as the prime suspect for the terrible explosion which ripped through the engine room as the flywheel disintegrated, bringing down the ruins of a golden age on the head of poor Walton Grinrod.

Nor was it to be expected that Percy Smallcroft, rather than run pictures in the special edition of the *Straggling Town Examiner* like the one he had of Red Eileen genuflecting before a pair of pinstriped royal trousers, should lead with the scene of devastation which was all that was left of the Balaclava Mill engine room, under the headline:

PRINCE ROCKED IN TERROR HORROR MILL NIGHTMARE!

The only thing which happened that was expected and universally welcomed was the sudden disappearance of Austin Perry along with any further plans to turn the Straggling Town into a tourist attraction. It was generally agreed, in discriminating circles like the taproom of the Pack o' Lies, that our past was better kept alive in the hearts and minds of those who had lived it, rather than put into the hands of heritage pipsqueaks from out of town who couldn't tell a shuttle from a picking stick.

Chapter Twenty-Three

Five Try Trainspotting

SOME THINK that nostalgia is the mildew of middle age, the first sign
that rot is setting in. But here in the Straggling Town we enjoy it. It's
probably because our golden age is past. That was the time when our mills
were all busy and we were helping to make the rest of England rich. Now
most of them have been pulled down and we have been forgotten, left
behind with our memories. But that's the way many of us prefer it, because
we don't hold with what's going on these days. We don't really understand
it. How can people be doing so well, driving round in new cars, taking
fancy foreign holidays, when nobody seems to be making anything anymore like we did? We still boast of Amos Hardacre's mill, where they
wove enough for the home market before breakfast, and the rest was for
export.

'What do they do there now?' asked little Jimmy Capstick, as puzzled
as the rest of us round the table at the Poet and Peasant.

'Weapons of mass destruction,' boomed Bag o' Nails in his best Old
Testament voice.

'What he means, I think,' explained Arthur, 'is that they make parts for
aircraft that can drop nuclear bombs.'

'But they can't do that!' cried Jimmy with a sudden passion which caused
more than one glass to be put down.

'I got a letter from the Council this morning for not paying my rates.
At the top of the page it has this picture of a pigeon and underneath it
says we're a Nuclear Free Zone!'

Next to the pint glasses on the table had appeared a large can of worms.

We did our level best to unravel them. Did the Council first make it
clear to Moscow or to Sadam Hussein or any other would-be nuclear-happy
maniac that we were to become a nuclear-free zone? Is there a map on the
wall somewhere in the Kremlin with a warning not to drop any bombs on
us in the Straggling Town? And just what were they doing making parts
for nuclear bombers in town? This nuclear-free business was beginning to

sound a bit like a chap who professes to be a vegetarian working in an abattoire.

We came to the conclusion that there was as much hypocritical nonsense around these days as there was twaddle talked in the Town Hall, so we returned to reminiscing about a bygone age when the world seemed a much cosier and safer place, if only because we didn't know half as much about what was going on.

'At night we used to climb onto the roof of Hardacre's mill,' recalled Jimmy Capstick with a chuckle. 'I remember the time we nearly got caught. Bobby Wilkinson chased us all the way to the railway embankment but we hid from him in our den.'

'Now that was something,' said Arthur, a misty look coming into his eyes. 'The railway.'

Steam trains thundering through the cutting, flames from the firebox flickering in the faces of the crew. The smell of smoke mingling with the smell of paraffin from the signal lamps. Moonlight glinting on the rails. The distant signals piercing the night, beckoning to a mysterious and exciting world beyond.

So complete was the spell cast by these memories of the railway of our youth, that when Arthur suggested that we should all go there that very night to see what it was like nowadays, nobody objected.

I suppose there's something rather ridiculous about middle aged men trying to behave like kids again. There are things you just can't do so well any more. You may be good at driving a car, but what about getting over a barbed wire fence? We blundered around in the dark and the air was rent with the sound of oaths and tearing clothing.

'Ouch!' yelled Arthur, leaving skin behind.

But there was a light in his eyes. The line by night had lost none of its magic. We stood by the track staring at the black mouth of the tunnel. The green signal winked at us and seemed to say, 'Right, lads. All clear for adventure.'

But then, suddenly it was panic stations.

'Bloody Hell!' gasped Bag o' Nails. 'There's a train coming!'

A dim yellow light flickered and wavered in the darkness of the tunnel. We watched it spellbound as it grew, silently but swiftly. Then the rails began to whisper and sing and all at once it was upon us, springing out of the mouth of the tunnel with a warning shriek like a wild beast. A great yellow-faced diesel engine, blunt and powerful with strange eyes in the top of its head and a growling roar that shook the earth. Like startled rabbits we dived for cover in the grass of the embankment. The waggons thunderd past sending violent shockwaves through the night air. Then another angry shriek and it was gone, its red tail light melting into the distance.

'Did you see it?' cried Bag o' Nails emerging from the undergrowth.

'See it?' yelled Jimmy Capstick, jumping up and down trying to shake off a vicious bramble that had attacked his leg. 'It damned nearly flattened us.'

'No,' croaked Bag o' Nails with that hunted Boris Karloff look of his. 'The coffins.'

The rest of us stared at him. Had he gone barmy? Or had he really regressed, believing we really were the Famous Five and had just seen the ghost train?

'What do you mean, coffins?' demanded Arthur hoarsely.

'Those containers,' explained Bag o' Nails. 'They were radioactive waste flasks. On the train.'

A sudden after-image, like the shadow burnt by the sun on the retina, blazed into the mind. Those square white chambers with ribs down the sides. Like nothing we'd ever seen before.

'How do you know?' I asked. It was a stupid question. Bag o' Nails was a walking X-file of official subterfuge.

We decided there was only one way to be sure. We'd visit the signal box and interrogate whoever was in there. We'd always wanted to go inside a signal box.

When the signalman saw us climbing his steps, we saw him blanch and rush to lock the door. He'd read about the great train robbers. Fortunately we recognised Ernest Plews and persuaded him to let us in.

'It's more than my job's worth if you're seen in here,' he complained.

'Your job'll not be worth anything after privatisation,' retorted Arthur sourly.

We squeezed what we wanted to know out of him.

'It's called the Sellafield Special,' he told us. 'There's another one scheduled for next Tuesday, late on.'

'Right', said Arthur, 'can we have a go at pulling the levers?'

For the next half-hour the lights changed so often you'd have thought Railtrack were holding a disco. An owl perched near one of the signals had to go back to bed with a headache.

The next day Arthur led a deputation to the Council. How could material that could end up in nuclear bombs be allowed to pass through a nuclear-free zone? Jobs, he was told by Councillor Horace Slack who had shares in the nuclear industry. Jobs and exports to make us great again.

In the back room of the Poet and Peasant Working Men's Club a daring plan of action was forged of which Julian, Dick, George, Anne, Timmy the dog and Greenpeace would have been proud.

The following Tuesday night, five boys aged around fifty-something crouched in a cutting not far from the tunnel waiting for the Sellafield Special. A plan to bribe signalman Plews with several bottles of Timothy Taylor's championship ale had failed to persuade him to leave the signal at red. Instead a twinkling green blithely beckoned humanity towards destruction. A somewhat more desperate alternative had had to be adopted, and the danger of it was written on all our faces.

'Let's just go home now,' pleaded Jimmy Capstick. 'We could be watching Football Extra.'

But it was too late. The flickering light had danced into the tunnel.

Jumping to his feet Bag o' Nails began furiously waving his flashlight at the oncoming train. The rest of us followed suit. It wasn't until it burst from the tunnel that we heard the screech of brakes. With an angry shudder the locomotive ground to a halt only feet from us.

It must have been Bag o' Nails' opening remark which convinced the driver that he'd come across a party of deranged midnight moth-catchers.

'We want you to turn round and go back,' he announced with no thought for how he was going to manage that.

In all the excitement we'd forgotten to discuss what we were going to say to the driver. Also, we'd calculated without the treachery of Ernest Plews, who was looking forward to free shares and a lucrative pension package after privatisation. For at that moment the night air was split with the sound of police sirens and the shadows burst to life with flashing blue lights.

We ran like we'd never run for years, making our escape into the woods. It was only afterwards, when our gashed shins and pulled muscles had healed, and when thoughts of being detained indefinitely at Her Majesty's pleasure had subsided, that we fully appreciated what a wonderful night we'd had. But then, it takes time to colour experience with that special rosy tint which eventually turns it, I suppose, into nostalgia.

Chapter Twenty-Four

An Immovable Objector

*T*HERE'S no irony intended when people who live here say that one of the best things about the Straggling Town is the ease with which you can get out of it. They are, of course, referring to all the wonderful countryside on our doorstep, in particular the high open moorland which fills our skyline. Some of us, ground down by the daily struggle of existence, may never find time to walk there. Indeed, we may rarely look up to follow with our eye the sweep of the hills unchanged since the lakes of ice scoured out our valley home before human time began. But we all know it's there, and it's an inviolable backcloth to our lives, giving us a sense of place in the natural scheme of things and awakening in us, whenever we care to renew our acquaintance with it, that ancient feeling of affinity with the land from which we all began.

Arthur and me, and the others, when we're not to be found sorting out life's vexations in the bar of the Poet and Peasant Working Men's Club, are quite likely to be spotted working off the effects of a jar or two by toiling up the steep valley sides before enjoying the exhiliration of a ramble on the moortops.

It was early summer, and after reaching the top we'd thrown ourselves down on the freshly greening grass to revel in the feel of the warm sun on our faces. The air was heavy with the hum of insects and larks rose and fell on columns of giddy song. The cadence of a curlew lapped over us like musical water, and high overhead islands of pure white cloud stretched towards infinity.

'Heaven,' breathed Arthur, and we felt the peace settle on us like a blessing.

But one man's heaven is another's business opportunity and our peace was broken by the sound of a car approaching along the track to the old driftmine.

We turned to watch one of those four-wheel drive vehicles draw up, those fashionable accessories of the Aga lout who likes to cultivate an image

of off-road adventurism but rarely takes them further than the local
cash-and-carry. It was aggressively fitted out with bull bars.

'Handy, if you bump into one of the local kangaroos,' observed Arthur
sourly.

Two men, suited under their spotless wax jackets stepped out and began
pointing like robber barons dividing their spoils. One waved a clipboard.

We groaned. Clipboards always spell trouble: traffic policemen about to
flag you down. Town planners with an eye to driving a motorway through
your allotment. A clipboard was as unwelcome on our moortop as the
yuppie who brandished it.

'Come on, let's clear off,' urged Arthur, wrinkling his nose at the smell
of Eau de Cologne.

'Hang on,' said Bag o' Nails, whose own nose was like early warning
radar. 'I want to know what they're up to.'

When we want to know something in the Straggling Town we just ask.
Strangers might not like it, and with the word-mincers from the South
we've got a reputation for rudeness. But we like to know where we stand
and then we can deal plainly with people. So Bag o' Nails sailed up to
them and asked them what they were up to. They were so taken aback,
he got his answer.

It was a body blow. A consortium of out of town businessmen, of which
the wafting clipboard and his crony were representatives, were to turn the
whole moortop into an open cast coal mine. The cry of the curlew was to
be replaced by the roar of an army of mechanical diggers as our little piece
of heaven was transformed into a hell on earth of towering slag heaps and
churning seas of coal dust. It would only be for ten years, explained the
waxed jackets reassuringly. Then it would all be filled in with waste and
landscaped and reseeded so that no one would know the difference.

'But you can't!' protested Arthur.

'We can,' they retorted with a blinding flash of gold fillings. 'We've
already got planning permission.' And they jumped back into their car and
drove off, their vehicle blowing a long raspberry of exhaust gas at us as it
disappeared.

Bag o' Nails called down the wrath of heaven upon their heads. Standing
there with the staff he always carried with him on our walks, he resembled
some vengeful magician, some dark custodian of our ancestral rights. And
he gave full vent to the morbid preoccupations of his imagination. Hadn't
he long been a student of human misfortune, in particular the misadventures
which had befallen those who had attempted to pillage these hills before?
The miners buried alive under collapsed roofs or lost forever in their maze

of airless underground galleries. Bag o' Nails knew of them all and laid their dire fate at the door of some jealous spirit of the hills that lurked within them or walked over them on nights when the wind howled, but above all wreaked horrid revenge on those who dared to disturb them.

The rest of us were much more concerned about how planning permission for this environmental outrage could have been passed, and we hurried back down to the Straggling Town to find out. It was the old story of a lack of public vigilance and planning officials all too happy to take advantage: a notice couched in obscure legalese hidden away on a page of the local paper no one ever reads. Similar ones pinned to telegraph poles for the wind to snatch and the rain to smear. Councillors like Horace Slack, chairman of planning, whose business interests ran deep and dark as old mine workings themselves. And Government connivance. For it appeared that unbeknown to us who live here, our moors had been officially designated an area for waste disposal and mining free-for-alls, a place for any Tom, Dick or Harry in a baseball cap with a clapped out JCB to rip up. The locals wouldn't notice, the officials from the South reasoned. After all, weren't we like the matchstick men in Lowry pictures, bent double, flat caps pulled down over our heads and too busy watching our straining whippets to notice what was happening to our hills, our sensibilities too shrivelled by working 'in t' mill' to care about our countryside?

Wrong. Wrong on every calumnious count.

Talking of calumnies, I myself have been guilty of one of the gravest. For a long time now I have mocked Hilda-the-Ton. It is too easy to laugh at fat people and assume that because of their appearance they must be stupid, ugly people inside. We are too ready to overlook that, underneath all that ponderous bulk, could lie a soul of exquisite sensitivity, a rare sense of beauty trembling to get out. And this turned out to be the case with Hilda-the-Ton.

No one felt more than Hilda the shock at the proposed rape of our moorland. How many have been the times when, hauling her troublesome frame about the town she has stopped to mop her brow and look up at the hills? And how her heart has danced. Fallen arches and varicose veins may have stopped her from climbing up there, but it did not stop her soul from reaching out, from winging its way like a summer butterfly between the nodding cotton grass. And there was something else hidden inside that heaving bosom. It was a giant resolve. Not the sort that could resist cream cakes or battered fish from Butterfield's. But a resolve to fight injustice, an inherited trait from a grandmother who had been a suffragette. Until now Hilda had given no clue of this. The only time she had burnt her bra was when it had no longer fitted.

But cometh the hour, cometh the woman.

It must have been a titanic struggle, but no one was around to witness it. Like the legendary Sisyphus, Hilda-the-Ton rolled her boulder-like body up the hill. How many times she stopped, rolled back again even, no one knows. But she succeeded, and this was bearing the additional burden of a large shopping bag.

The first we heard about it was from Percy Smallcroft at the local paper. 'There was a demonstration on the moortop against the mining', he announced. Soon, half the Straggling Town were puffing their way up there. And what a sight met our eyes. Waxed jackets all over the place, like agitated dung beetles, bellowing into mobile phones. Hulking workmen looking on in a mixture of fear and admiration. And at the centre of it all, Hilda-the-Ton sitting on the ground chained to a large bulldozer and blithely making her way through a bag of coconut macaroons.

It may have been the bad publicity which frightened the mining company away. Tabloid pictures of Hilda's stupendous frontage squaring up to one of the machines under the headline:

BUXOM HILDA IN BULLDOZER BUST-UP!

On the other hand, it may have been the large number of mechanical breakdowns which finally got rid of the clipboards. Bag o' Nails, who had taken to walking around with a monkeywrench concealed in his pocket, blamed the latter on the vengeful guardian of the moor purging his kingdom of despoilers. Whatever it was, all copies of the map of the area in the hands of planners now show a large red patch marked, 'Sensitive Area. Do Not Touch.'

Chapter Twenty-Five

Filthy Lucre

As far as money is concerned I think it's fair to say that there's a certain amount of tight-handedness about the Straggling Town. Whether it's to do with our proximity to Yorkshire where, I'm told, they're born with their hands in their pockets, I don't know. But like other places where most folk work for a wage and have to rely on the generosity of their employers, there's not a lot of money about. If we can keep our heads above water we count ourselves lucky. We might even be floating backwards, but so long as we don't sink no one complains. The spectre of the workhouse still lurks not so far beneath the surface of our tribal memory and we're grateful that the Government hasn't got round to reintroducing the idea, yet.

One of the most obvious signs of this carefulness is our prowess as hoarders. I don't know anyone here in the Straggling Town who isn't a hoarder of one thing or another. Red Eileen has enough tins of sockeye salmon salted away in her larder to put even the famous grocer of Grantham's daughter to shame. Hilda-the-Ton has enough fents from her days as a weaver, when she used to smuggle them home under her pinny, to stock a Karachi bazaar. And Bag o' Nails regularly predicts there'd be enough of everything for human progress to continue uninterrupted for whoever survived inside it.

We found him in there the other day. It isn't so much one building as a concretion. Like a termite (or is it a dung beetle?), Bag o' Nails was forever adding bits on. It had set out in life as one of those covered goods waggons painted in LMS red that you sometimes see on allotments and places miles away from the nearest railway. How they got there is a mystery, involving human ingenuity every bit as great as in the construction of Stonehenge. But stuck on everywhere, like some bizarre and delapidated lego, were a series of sheds and lean-tos made out of whatever impromptu building materials could be cadged or half-inched within transporting distance. Tongued and grooved boarding, often with floral bedroom wallpaper still attached, merged with corrugated iron and tea-chests.

Rain-swollen chipboard coexisted happily with ancient metal adverts announcing, 'Bile Beans Are The Best!' It was a medley of materials which comprised a sociological history of the century to say nothing of a work of art. I shouldn't be surprised if one day someone in a bow tie from the Tate Gallery came along and bought it lock, stock and kitchen sink and put it on display there. Not that everyone appreciates it. The local council has dished out more nuisance notices than a bilious traffic warden, and the neighbours – for it's right behind Bag o' Nails' house – are always complaining to the local paper. One recent letter described it as reminiscent of the worst excesses of a Sao Paulo ghetto. Now who in the Straggling Town ever gets to Sao Paulo? ('We're thinking of trying Brazil this year, Fred's getting tired of Minehead.')

But if the outside was a hotch potch it was nothing compared to what met your eyes when you stepped inside and made your way through its labyrinth of annexes. Next to a glass case containing a stuffed polecat was a mildewed dressmaking bust for outsized ladies, complete with pins. There was a dentist's drill which looked as if it had been used by Dr Mengale. There were hand grenades and mangles, trouser presses and home enema kits. You could pick up a set of drain rods or a sun ray lamp. No one in the Straggling Town needed to get rid of anything because a part had broken. Its replacement, like a dusty doppleganger, was hidden away in one of the hundreds of sets of drawers and cupboards. It was a museum to the time-tested local precept: Throw nowt away because you never know when it might come in useful, and, in any case, one day it might be worth a bob or two. But you couldn't help but think, as you picked your way amongst rusted shoe lasts and 7-inch TV sets complete with magnifiers, that if everyone in the land shared this hoarding instinct life would soon grind to a halt, gridlocked under its own lumber. But here, where obsolescence was a dirty word, Bag o' Nails was as happy as a bower bird, or as happy as a man can be who insists on purifying his own tapwater and carrying iodine tablets in case of nuclear attack.

He was busy at a workbench, fiddling with something you and I would have pitched in the dustbin sooner than look at.

'Now then, lads, what can I do for you?' he said with a gleam in his dark eye which spotted cash. This, after all, was his shop, where his moth and rust corrupted treasures could be turned into money.

'Just a social call,' I said, and watched the gleam snuff out like a miser's candle.

But he wasn't long without a customer. The sound of clogs and an unmistakable whiff of shippon soon interrupted our conversation. A small

man with the disshevelled look of a victimised hen had arrived. It was
Reuben Moorhead, a farmer from off the moor and a renowned skinflint.
We settled back to watch blood being squeezed from stone.

Reuben was after a part for his tractor, an ugly and temperamental beast
which some reckoned was so old it had solid wheels and once appeared in
a Thomas Hardy film. With barely a pause for thought, just a quick mental
rummage in the astonishing filing cabinet that he kept between his ears,
Bag o' Nails was into one of the drawers and emerging with the replacement.

''ow much?' asked Reuben, with that feined disinterest familiar to
observers of his kind at livestock auctions.

'It's yours for a fiver,' said Bag o' Nails, as if they were in great demand
and he was doing him a favour.

Reuben reacted as if he'd been kicked in the solar plexis by a donkey.

'A fiver?' he gasped. 'What good is it to you?'

'What good is a shelf full of pickled gherkins to Mr Safeway?' replied
Bag o' Nails, with a surprising understanding of retail marketing. 'Business
is business.'

We watched them haggle like camel traders until eventually a price was
struck. Neither man looked happy. In fact, Reuben Moorhead seemed ready
to burst into tears. Could he be so hard up? A poor farmer sounded as
improbable as a cow with wings. But we were not prepared for what
happened next.

With a furtive glance into the shadows around us, as if to check for
lurking muggers or concealed tax inspectors, the farmer hitched up his
greasy dufflecoat and dug into his back pocket. He removed a wad of
banknotes as thick as the London telephone directory.

Arthur whistled. 'Loose change, Reuben?' he said.

The farmer snarled like a dog with a bone and peeled off a grubby note.
For all the pleasure it afforded him he could have been peeling off a slice
of his own skin.

'Don't trust banks,' he growled. 'Don't trust nobody.' And stowing away
his cash he picked up his purchase and was gone.

'I wonder where he keeps it, then?' I said, entertaining criminal thoughts.

Bag o' Nails had been peering closely at the note for signs of counter-
feiting and his nose wrinkled. 'He's probably got a spare charnel house,'
he said. 'Smell that,' and he handed it over.

'Pooh!' cried Arthur, after giving it a good sniff. 'It stinks like a poke
o' devils.'

You don't need to know what a poke o' devils is to know what it smells
like. Let's put it this way, if all money smelt like that, banknotes would

have to carry a Government health warning – not a bad idea when you come to think of it. Even the Queen looked to be turning her nose up at this one.

It became a recurrent source of speculation as to where Reuben Moorhead kept his money. So much so that we took to walking past his farmhouse on our walks just to see if we could get any clues. His farm was the outdoor equivalent of Bag o' Nails' Ark, only knee-deep in manure.

'You wouldn't know where to start to look,' said Arthur.

But at that moment we spotted Reuben bending over a grate.

'Watch,' whispered Arthur suddenly, and we crouched behind a silage bale.

The farmer was tugging away at a rope which disappeared into a drain. When it emerged there was a large plastic provender bag attached to the end. After a quick look around he unwrapped it and transferred the contents of his back pocket swiftly into the sack. Then he lowered it back down the drain.

But just at that moment a rather muddy goose waddled its way round the corner of the barn and seeing us, let out the most dreadful cackling. In a movement that would have done credit to Clint Eastwood, Reuben Moorhead swung round, grabbed his shotgun from where it had been leaning against the house wall, and discharged two barrels into the silage bale. We fled in panic to the sound of rapid reloading.

We decided it would be in no one's interests to reveal the location of Reuben Moorhead's safe-deposit arrangements. Blood would most certainly have been shed. And no amount of filthy lucre was worth that.

Chapter Twenty-Six

Fossils Aroused

I WOULDN'T like you to get the impression that we in the Straggling Town are stuck in some kind of time warp, that we're like those fossil creatures that you can pick up on the beach at Whitby, snugly curled up inside their stone shells as the tides of time wash over them. If there's anything petrified about our way of life it's for a very good reason. Frankly, we feel rather let down by progress. We sometimes think the world is going backwards.

Take knocking things down. We've had more of that than Frank Bruno. They've laid into our old methodist chapels like heathens. Fine old stones soaked in prayers and 'Onward Christian Soldiers!' have gone to make ballast for motorways. One of our chapels has been converted into a bingo hall and another has become the Mount Zion Video Centre, selling such lurid offerings as *Saucy Ingar's Swedish Capers* and *The Creature from the Crypt*. Our forefathers must be shaking in their family vaults. Only the other week Bag o' Nails was moved to write on their window in felt tip, 'Remember Gomorrah!'

And then there's the memorial hospital, paid for out of public subscription and near empty purses. More gallstones have been removed in there and more red and crinkled babies slapped into life than there are shrimps in Morecambe Bay. But what has become of it now to ease our pain and bring delight? A tarmac roundabout and Little Glutton roadside diner, dispensing matchstick thin chips in cardboard cups and deep-fried chicken litter nuggets. If this is progress Yorkshire's full of philanthropists.

But the latest act of civic sacrilege strikes at the very heart and soul of life in the Straggling Town. A proposal to knock down our dear old market hall and replace it with a shopping centre, complete with fountain, palm trees and piazza around which dazed looking families of consumers can wander dressed as if ready for the beach at Magaluf. Well, that was the picture given by the artist's impression of the development printed on the front page of the *Straggling Town Examiner* the morning the news broke.

The market hall was abuzz with the indignation of a swarm of bees who have returned to find their hive being dismantled.

Most venomous of all was the criticism that came from the central table in the Cosy Cafe. It curdled the malt vinegar.

'Just lead me to the man who's behind all this,' snarled Red Eileen, sinking her teeth into a chocolate eclair and leaving a ghastly smear of crimson lipstick on the pastry.

Fred Chadwick the butcher was feeding steak into his mincer and long worms of glistening meat were growing from the end. 'They're trying to squeeze us out, that's what they're trying to do,' he said from between his teeth.

Across the way, Her-from-the-Tripe-Stall jabbed her fork into a piece of tripe which was basking in the juice of a white enamel tray and flipped it onto some grease-proof paper. Her customer, an anaemic creature who was known to eat nothing else but tripe and buttered creamcrackers, cast a connoisseur's eye over the other dishes in which the pale mysteries of the cow's wonderful stomach were laid out, some grey, some yellow, some prettily ruched like bonnet trimmings. 'And I'll 'ave a nice piece of helder for our Halbert,' she said.

All these esoteric delights under threat. The stalls of crumpets, of stew and hard, the roll mops and ham shanks, the prize-winning black puddings and the pies. Oh the Pickup's pies! The marrowfat peas waiting to be mushed, the sausages you could trust. The blood drinks and genuine dandelion and burdock. All the traditional fare that refreshes the parts no boil-in-the-bag can ever reach.

Over at the knicker stall, out of bounds to men, where ladies of a more generous circumference can still find satisfaction, a similar cry of lamentation could be heard between the noisy thwack of elastic as products were tested. Where else could whalebone still be found to curb the wilful flesh and shore up the bastions of moral decency in a degenerate age? Not in the chainstore flimsies wantonly on display and 'giving men ideas.'

And on the wetfish stall, Fleetwood Norman, whetting his blade like Shylock, unzipped the innards from a silent haddock and mused murderously on town hall planning officials.

The same subject was occupying our minds as we stood outside Clegg's ironmongers stall where they still sold segs you could nail to the soles of your gardening boots and extend their life for another year. We had our suspicions about who might be behind the plan and the arrival of Percy Smallcroft from the *Examiner* gave us the chance to confirm them.

'I'm not sure that I'm in a position to reveal my sources,' said the pompous little hack, puffing out his chest like a pigeon. Translated this meant, 'What's in it for me?'

Arthur patted his back pocket and the hack's eyes lit up.

'What did I tell you?' cried Arthur after he'd gone. 'Horace Slack.'

Now I think it's true to say that in the Straggling Town there's not a great deal of ambition about. It's usually the case where people are contented with their lot. Well-balanced people, who like where they live and generally get along with their neighbours, don't spend all hours God sends plotting and conniving to get richer. This is the carrot stuck out by those who run the consumer society and try to make us restless only to make themselves richer. Councillor Horace Slack was one such person. He'd no friends except the ones he bought, and unfortunately there were one or two of those about in the town hall.

The public gallery of the town hall was packed when the Council sat to discuss the plan to develop the market. Under portraits of grisled and ermined aldermen the members sat trying to look dignified and intelligent while Councillor Slack outlined his vision of the new market place. The stallholders need have no fear. A special arcade was to be built for them where they could continue to ply their trade dressed in traditional clogs and shawls, striped aprons and straw boaters. It would be a great hit and bring lots of money in from out of town.

'Fossils,' came a strident cry from the gallery. 'Does he think we're all fossils?'

All heads turned. Red bouffant flashing, eyes darting fire, Red Eileen stood shaking her fist at Horace Slack. An explosive mixture of menace and allure, it was a sight to ignite the most primal instincts of any male, and the effect on the Councillor was instantaneous. Many have been unmanned by the Red One. Three husbands could testify to the destructive violence of her charms, only their lips are forever sealed with clay in the Straggling Town cemetery. Councillor Slack, his speech unfinished, sank back into his seat, his knees shaking, his face blanched as tripe. The very stuffing of his ambition lay scattered at his feet and only one thought now filled his being. For the rest of the meeting he sat unable to take his eyes off her.

Afterwards a liveried official was instructed to deliver a sealed envelope of an extremely confidential nature to Red Eileen. Much later that evening, the mayoral limousine, its pennant judiciously removed but the registration mark ST 1 leaving no doubt as to its origin, slid noiselessly into Disraeli Street and Eileen herself, dressed to massacre the entire male population, was ushered into its soft leather interior and whisked away to attend a small and highly intimate soirée in the mayor's parlour. In fact, along with copious quantities of vodka and tomato juice, generously provided at the ratepayers' expense. Events were reaching an amicable climax between the two when they were interrupted by the sudden arrival of a third party in the rotund shape of Percy Smallcroft, complete with camera and flashlight. Just how he'd got to know about the meeting is a mystery, and being the professional that he is, leg irons would not get him to reveal his sources. But it was soon made known to Councillor Slack that the pictures he had taken would be available at the Mount Zion Video Centre, under the counter of course, if the Councillor was not immediately prepared to drop all plans for converting our precious market into a shopping mall. This, I'm glad to say, he did, and we were able to creep back happily into our shells with at least one of our public buildings spared the dubious benefits of progress.

Chapter Twenty-Seven

The Proof of the Pie

*U*NLESS you've actually experienced it, it's hard to imagine the lift to the spirits which occurs around quarter to ten every morning barring Sundays in the Straggling Town. Life anywhere can have its grey patches, when the joy and excitement is bleached out by failure and disappointment, and fun is in as short supply as bacon butties at a bar mitzvah. Then you've just got to sit it out and wait for the sunshine to return. But we're lucky. Our sun rises every morning around quarter to ten. I am, of course, referring to the time when the first batch of Pickup's pies arrive from the bakery.

By half past nine you can sense the expectation. In every workplace lists have been drawn up on the backs of envelopes and production surges like the power supply as everyone puts their back into it to make the time pass quickly until the pies arrive. And on the market people start to arrive like parched wildebeests to a watering hole. They mill around looking at their watches or waiting for the chimes of the Town Hall clock.

'He's late today,' says someone, shuffling impatiently. But Fred Pickup is usually as punctual as a parson. The cry goes up, 'T' pies are 'ere!' and there's a regular stampede as everyone rushes for the pie stall. Fred appears with the first of the trays and the heavenly aroma swirls amongst us like an ambrosial mist. Gastric juices which have stayed sluggish since first light and resolutely failed to be moved by the breakfast offering of toast and marmalade, now run amock like a stream in spate. It's not unheard of, especially on a Monday when the previous day's abstinence has sharpened the craving, for scuffles to break out. Then, Red Eileen's knitting needles, whose steel points poke dangerously through the crocheted sides of her shopping bag, jab into life and order is restored.

Always at the head of the queue is our very own answer to Piltdown Man, Jurassic Jeff. If you are what you eat, Jeff is a Pickup's pie. Round, with a glazed skull and a hole where a brain should be. He cut his baby teeth on their crusts and has not been without one for a day ever since, that's if you exclude an ill-fated trip to Benidorm when he lay for a fortnight in a darkened room listlessly sipping lager and suffering from withdrawal symptoms. His daily quota is between four and six, depending on the state of his stomach from the night before and the arrival of his Giro. This may sound excessive to the brown rice and lentil brigade and anyone benighted enough not to have tasted a Pickup's pie. But Jeff is built like a concrete mixer. His chest is so vast his arms won't rest at his sides but stick out as if ready to crush you. They're tattooed with dripping daggers and snarling serpents. Police horses stay in their stables on football match days when he's around and nothing can coax them out. And on days like today no one disputed his right to be at the front of the queue.

But despite his formidable appearance, to see Jurassic Jeff deal with a Pickup's pie was to witness an act of the utmost delicacy and finesse. You see, at a quarter to ten in the morning, a Pickup's pie is as tender and fragile as a new-laid egg. Straight from the oven, its pastry shell has still not had time to adjust to the brusque fingers of the air, and its fragrant juices are still warm and fluent, a heavenly distillation barely ready for coarse human handling.

'Mind you don't bust 'em,' warned Her-from-the-Pie-Stall as she always did when she handed over the bag.

Now it was Jurassic Jeff's custom to dispatch a couple of the pies there and then. It was a ritual which served only to heighten the craving of the rest of the queue, and to observe it was to be made aware that poetry can enter even the most savage breast. Removing a pie from the bag, Jeff raised it to his mouth and nibbled away at the crust with the fastidiousness of a bumble bee gnawing its way through a petunia petal. Then, tilting back his head he drained the rich juices in one, giving out such a sigh of content, you'd have thought his team had just carried off the FA cup. He then polished off the rest of the pie, and just to show he'd not gone soft, let out a burb that shook the awning over the pie stall.

Now there are many who might scoff at the fuss we make of our humble Pickup's pie. These are the people who might pass through our town and pity us. 'Where are their restaurants and theatres?' they cry with a shudder. 'How could anyone live here with so few civilising amenities?' But our Pickup's pie is a civilising amenity, along with our pint of Old Rapture and our freedom to roam the ancient hills of our birth. These to us are worth a dozen bijou bistros or arid concert halls. What we eat, where we live and who we are, we would swap with no one. We reckon that in any league table for the quality of life, we're streets ahead of anyone else. But what we didn't yet know was that that quality of life was under threat. Our precious pies were poised to disappear.

Fred Pickup's health was poor. That pallor we'd begun to notice wasn't just flour, though it was probably due to its effects. Forty years with your head in a mixing bowl of watercrust pastry has its occupational hazards. Just as coaldust settles on a miner's lungs so can flour on a baker's. And then there were the early hours. Up before dawn to light the ovens, cutting and blocking, boiling trotters to make that rich lip-gluing jelly. All the unseen brushstrokes that went to complete the finished masterpiece, all had taken their toll. Fred Pickup's doctor had told him: 'Give up now, before it's too late.'

But Fred had a responsibility to his customers, to the town. Pickup's pies had been made in the Straggling Town since 1893. They had helped us to survive outbreaks of typhoid, cholera and world wars. Their nourishing properties had built the resilience required to survive unemployment and the weather. Mortality rates were significantly lower in the Straggling Town than in other places where their pies were found wanting. Someone had to be found to take over the business, and this was where the problem lay.

The recipe had been passed down from father to son now for four generations. The only time it was written down was when a father felt that the hour of his departure was near. Fred's own father had left it until he was on his deathbed. Then he had asked for a pencil and a piece of rice paper and had copied it out, in particular the subtle details of the unique seasoning which was always made up by him in secret behind locked doors. Then Fred had been instructed to go away and memorise it before swallowing the rice paper. Fred himself, alas, was childless, apart from a daughter who had been lost to him ever since she married a chartered accountant and went to live in Dorking. The future of the pie was hopeless unless someone could be found to continue the great tradition.

He'd made one or two discreet enquiries at a nearby catering college. But the only sort of pie today's students were interested in was something known as the cost accounted pie. It didn't matter what you put into it so long as it was cheap and made a handsome profit.

Fred finally came and opened his heart to us in the Poet and Peasant Working Men's Club. We were stunned at the prospect of the loss of a local institution, one more inroad from the grey tide of uniformity sweeping our island. Jurassic Jeff took it worst. He sat at the bar with his pint untouched looking as if he was going to cry. Finally it was he who broke the long hopeless silence.

'Do you think I could take over, Mr Pickup?' he said meekly.

It was not as daft as it sounded. Hadn't he a prodigious practical knowledge of the product? Didn't he once lecture us for a full hour on

Pies I Have Known, with examples from as far afield as Torquay and Gateshead gleaned from his travels as a football supporter? He had tasted the worst along with the best and lived to tell the tale.

It was agreed that Fred should take Jeff under his wing, so to speak. For a whole month no one saw him. Before dawn he disappeared into the bakery, only to emerge long after nightfall. Then, one day at a quarter to ten, flour coating his tattooes and a blob of setting pastry stuck to his earring, he appeared on the market. He wore a bashful smile and was bearing a tray full of pies. 'I made these,' he said.

Everyone took a leaf out of Jeff's old book and had a pie there and then. First a discreet nibble, then a tilt to savour the juices, then the rest, consumed in studious silence punctuated only by the occasional clack of false teeth and the odd over exuberent slurp. Poor Jeff was on tenterhooks, knotting his huge feet and peering at his great arms as if he'd just discovered a tattoo he'd never noticed before.

Then suddenly a great roar went up.and people were slapping him on the back. They would have hoisted him into the air had this been humanly possible. A new heir to the Pickup pie dynasty had been found and the Straggling Town let out a huge sigh of relief.

Chapter Twenty-Eight

There be Dragons!

*H*ERE in the Straggling Town we're surrounded by history. But it's of a very shadowy kind. There are no castles or stately homes where knights jousted and lords and ladies dallied. The fate of kings never hung on what happened here. If the history books are to be believed we weren't discovered until the industrial revolution came along and plucked us from our maypoles on the village green and ground us into work fodder in the dark Satanic mills. But history books don't tell you everything and we know different. We know that long before books were written people settled here. We've found their flints and arrowheads, their stone circles up on Ringstone hill and the strange mounds and tumuli where their chieftains lie sleeping. And we have our legends to prove it.

'She could be lying right under us now,' said Arthur Wormwell in a hushed voice.

We'd climbed to the top of Warcock Hill where the Vikings are said to have flown their fearsome battle standard, the raven. Now only jackdaws squabble around the outcrops of millstone grit. It's a wonderful vantage point. On a clear day you can see almost as far as the sea to the west, and to the east the moors rise to form the great watershed of England. The main road winds its way through the straggling valley, bringing the summer's first flush of day-trippers in their coaches in search of history and adventure and a good cup of tea and a home-made cake.

'I wonder what she was like?' said Arthur, turning onto his elbow and gazing at the mound where we were sitting. He patted a patch of dark green moss and watched the orange spores spring back like a miniature army of spears.

He was talking about our own Dark Age answer to Boadicea, a warrior chief of the Brigantes known as the Dragon Queen, who is said to have made the life of the invading Romans such a misery that all they could dream of was being back home flexing their pectorals on the beach at Rimini.

'If she ever existed,' growled Bag o' Nails.

'Oh, she existed all right,' replied Arthur. 'Women have always ruled in the Straggling Town. There's not a woman born and bred here that doesn't share some of her blood. Fighters they are. Six looms and six kids and a husband always down at the pub. How do you think they survived without iron in their hearts?'

This was said with some conviction, and those of us who knew Arthur's mum knew why. In fact, if the truth be told, and this is not history so I might as well, there wasn't one of us who didn't bear the scars of apron strings: home birds with a bit of a fear of stronger women, and showing a marked reluctance, despite the grey hairs, to grow up.

'You can forget your legends. I'd like to see some proof,' said Bag o' Nails.

'I'm not so sure about that,' said Arthur thoughtfully, spotting another charabanc nosing its way along the valley road. 'If there was something to be seen, imagine these moortops crawling with sightseers stopping off on their way from the Nora Batty tearooms to Camelot. You wouldn't be able to move for stalls selling woad-dyed t-shirts and dragonburgers. Sometimes history's better off left in the mind.'

A curlew let up a plaintive cry and we were all glad of the peace and solitude.

'You know,' went on Arthur, 'a chief would be buried along with her possessions. Priceless treasure may be inches from us.'

Jimmy Capstick shook his head. 'Nah. This is Reuben Moorhead's land,' he said, referring to the skinflint farmer. 'If there's owt worth anything here, he'd have sniffed it out long ago like a pig sniffs truffles.'

But the mention of treasure had got Bag o' Nails interested. There was nothing he'd like better to hoard and gloat over in that shed of his, especially if it was something snatched from under the nose of Reuben Moorhead. 'We should do a dig. We could come at night when Moorhead's not about,' he said.

Arthur frowned. He didn't like the way things were going. 'What about the curse?' he said suddenly.

Nobody had heard about a curse.

'I mean, look at Howard Carter,' went on Arthur, causing Jimmy Capstick to turn round and scan the skyline for approaching figures. 'The ancients had their ways of protecting the resting places of their leaders.'

Bag o' Nails stirred uncomfortably, as if he'd just discovered that he might be sitting on an anthill.

'Over them I shall set a guardian,' Arthur boomed, in what was meant to sound like the voice of a vengeful druid.

Just then a cloud covered the sun and we felt a cold edge to the breeze.

But Bag o' Nails had scented plunder and wasn't going to be put off that easily. The next day he appeared at the Poet and Peasant with what we took to be a vacuum cleaner wrapped in a black binliner.

'It's the home help,' cried Jimmy Capstick. 'Can't you wait till we've drunk up?'

Bag o' Nails fished the contraption out of its bag. 'Have you lot never seen a metal detector before? This is going to make us rich and the Straggling Town famous.' And he outlined his plan to use it to dig buried treasure out of Warcock Hill.

We left it until the night of the full moon. Blundering around on the moors in total darkness was no joke and flashlights were banned because of Reuben Moorhead's well-known shoot-to-kill policy with suspected sheep rustlers.

We struggled up the steep clough which led onto the moortop. The night air magnified every sound. Empty beech mast cases exploded underfoot like rifle shots. Somewhere far off a fox barked cold and clear and a farm dog answered. Overhead an owl let out a sudden shriek which set the hairs on our necks stirring. Age-old instincts were abroad and high above us the moon flitted amongst the trees wondering at our presumption in being there so late at night.

'We're journeying back in time,' whispered Arthur, capturing the mood.

'Not 'alf,' said Jimmy Capstick, 'Look!'

He was pointing at a tree. Stained with age and covered with lichen but still plainly visible were initials carved inside a heart pierced by a dripping arrow.

'That's your name,' cried Jimmy gleefully, addressing Arthur. If the moon hadn't hidden behind a cloud just then we might have seen him blush.

'And who was the girl?'

Arthur ignored the question. 'We used to come up here a lot when we were kids,' he said.

He was right. These woods were our playground. No computer games, not even a telly. Did it make us different? More in touch with the old gods?

Arthur put his hands around a tree trunk as if feeling for a warm pulse. The spirits of the place were entering him.

'They carried her up here,' he said. 'Her body on a stretcher plaited with willows. They came by night just like us, torchlight on their painted sweating faces. Their priests leading the way. Chanting. Winding up the spell.'

'You're barmy,' said Jimmy Capstick nervously.

Up ahead something stirred. The dead bracken crackled like ancient parchment. A shadow melted into the night.

'A wild animal,' said Arthur. Bag o' Nails bit his lip.

We broke through the trees onto the moortop and out into the pagan moonlight. The earth looked sickly and as we stumbled over the uneven ground pale moonshadows dodged after us. Overhead the moon had reddened the clouds like ironstone and the distant hills crouched black and menacing. Sheep watched us pass, raising their horned headdresses like ragged warriors.

'Look,' whispered Arthur suddenly. 'It's gone!'

Down below, the Straggling Town was lost in a shroud of mist. Not a light twinkled. Nothing to anchor us to the present. It was as if we had walked out of our time into the twilight of history.

'This is it,' hissed Arthur like a man in a trance. 'We're back. We've joined them.'

'Ooh,' cried Jimmy Capstick. 'I think I want to go home.'

But we'd reached the mound and Bag o' Nails, paler than ever in the moonlight, switched on his metal detector with a trembling hand.

'What if Reuben hears us?' whimpered Jimmy.

'Better the devil you know,' replied Arthur ominously.

Suddenly the machine began to bleep.

'Got something,' cried Bag o'Nails, and losing no time plunged his trowel into the ground.

The moment he did so the earth let out a blood-curdling shriek and Bag o' Nails shot back as if he'd been electrocuted.

Rising out of an island of reeds in front of us, arms outstretched as if to call down the wrath of heaven stood a ghastly apparition. It seemed fused out of molten moonlight, apart from its head which was a blazing halo of red. The blood-red lips wore an expression of the utmost malice.

'It's her, the Dragon Queen,' gulped Bag o' Nails, and dropping his metal-detector he fled. Jimmy Capstick already had twenty yards start on him.

'How did you manage to persuade Red Eileen to do it?' I asked afterwards.

Arthur grinned sheepishly. 'I threatened to reveal what we used to get up to in the woods when we were younger. She had quite a reputation for leading the lads on.'

'A good leader, eh?' I said.

Arthur nodded. 'Yes, and she made a pretty good Dragon Queen, don't you think? Enough to scare off the tourists. Just like we did the Romans.'

Chapter Twenty-Nine

Back from the Brink

*I*T CAME AS A SHOCK to everyone when Jack Stansfield was taken badly. He was as much a feature of the Straggling Town as one of the outcrops of millstone grit which look down on us from the hill tops: kindly in the comfortable way familiar landmarks are, but strong and, above all, permanent. He'd been around for as long as the longest memory could remember, his jovial laugh ringing out like the chimes of the town hall clock and his home-brewed brand of wisdom and common sense free to everyone in need of it. It was inconceivable that our Jack, as large and loud as life itself, should falter.

As ever, Bag o' Nails was first with the bad news. He burst in on us in the bar at the Poet and Peasant like an Atlantic front, a cold dampener on our jolly ritual.

'Stroke,' he pronounced, like a death knell. 'They found him slumped over in his greenhouse, seedlings everywhere. He'd been pricking out primulas. There's no hope.'

It is one of the least attractive sides of our natures here in the Straggling Town that we are a bit too willing to think the worst, to box people up before checking for any vital signs. It's probably a lot to do with our background: living in a valley where the sun is a stranger and rain clouds have the habit of anchoring themselves for days on end to the surrounding hilltops. And then there were the mills and their mean-eyed bosses, who did their best to drain the colour out of our lives. In and out of recession, we got into the habit of looking over our shoulders wondering where the next body blow was coming from. That was where Jack Stansfield was so different. He seemed to thrive off adverse conditions, like one of his Alpines. He would turn round, stick his chin out and say, 'We've had set-backs before. We'll survive,' and off he'd sail through the choppiest seas. Jack was an inspiration.

But Bag o' Nails' news brought a wake-like atmosphere to the club and we began to discuss him as if he'd already gone.

who had fallen foul of authority had once fled to save their lives. The men and women who had stood up against cruel bosses and narrow-minded neighbours, who had dared to shout 'Stuff your job!' or 'I will marry the one I love.' Those who had cried 'Respectability be damned!' and had taken life by the scruff of the neck and squeezed out as much passion and roistering good fun as they could get.

And the dried-up pen-pushers, the lap-top lapdogs to the south had forgotten that the same red blood of rebellion still ran in our veins today. And that this time, by trying to close down our market, they'd pushed us around once too often. This was the last straw.

'Off with 'em!' cried Red Eileen, brandishing the big, flat-bladed knife Her-from-the-Tripe-Stall used to slice up chitterlings. The glint from the blade was nothing compared to the murderous gleam in the Red One's eyes. The afternoon sunlight shone on her henna beehive hair-do so that it looked for all the world like a copper helmet. Few needed to be reminded that a thousand years before, Eric Bloodaxe had passed this way bestowing his heroic seed upon the local peasant girls.

News of the sale had just broken, and the mood on the market was ugly. One caucus of discontent was focused around the Cosy Cafe where an assortment of Straggling Town matrons, looking as crusty as the rims on the brown sauce bottles, were painting a nightmare picture of mealtimes under the catering regime of the Moneygrab supermarket chain.

'Slimy 'am,' cried Her-from-Next-Door, pulling a face like a vat of malt vinegar.

'Injected it is,' hissed Hilda-the-Ton. 'Full of salt and water.'

'Not real 'am,' said Fred Chadwick the butcher's wife, who knew about such things. And she lent forward like a witness to spare-part surgery at the General Hospital. 'Tails and toenails. Eyeballs and nostrils. They all go in. Even the grunt.' And spotting a degree of incredulity in her audience, she added. 'Can't be real. There's no bone.' And a vision of slimy, boneless pigs bereft of their eyeballs, slithering around like pink jellyfish, seized the rapt minds.

The menfolk had gathered around Pillings ironmonger's stall, a more fitting location for life's menders of broken yardbrushes and screwers up of pothooks. The conversation was all about the venality of D-I-Y superstores who only sold lightbulbs in threes and wouldn't split a pack of screws.

'And them assistants know nowt,' pronounced Bag o' Nails like the hanging judge. 'Can't tell a bradawl from a gimlet,' he sneered. And I vowed to go away and look them both up in the dictionary on peril of losing my credibility as a male.

But these were men who not only patched leaking troughings and greased backyard snecks; they were warriors. Hard, maybe, now to discern in their Oxfam cardigans and Tommy Ball trainers. But these men stood in an unbroken line from the Brigante tribesmen who had painted their naked torsos in woad and rattled their wooden spears from the top of Ingleborough and put the wind up the invading Roman legions. Who'd faced the wrath of the Scots at Bannockburn and chased the poncy cavaliers from Marston Moor. Who'd been slaughtered like lambs in the mud of Passchendaele. So what terrors did a few town hall bureaucrats with shiny breacher-bottoms hold for them?

'What you going to do, then?' demanded Percy Smallcroft, shaking the ink down into the tip of his Biro and thumbing through a grubby notebook to find a clean page. This was Percy's biggest story since the discovery of a cannabis factory in the Parks Department potting shed. His editor had given him strict instructions to show no sympathy for any opposition to the superstore. Moneygrab would be taking out weekly full-page adverts for their eyeball burgers and fish-fin fingers in the *Examiner*. Their battery eggs may taste of fishmeal but for some people they were golden eggs.

And one of these was Councillor Horace Slack, chairman of the Planning Committee that was overseeing the new superstore development, and by one of those amazing coincidences that are so remarkably common in the affairs of towns up and down the land, just happened to own the land surrounding the market where a four-acre car park for the superstore was planned, and was just negotiating a selling price with the company that would make the Channel tunnel look like value for money. But who knows if that will ever come out in the wash – as the housewife said who'd just washed her husband's overalls with his pay-packet in the pocket. What was of more immediate concern to us was how to save our market, to stop it disappearing into the history books like the cannon ball and the clay pipe.

'Me segs for me gardening boots,' wailed Bag o' Nails.

'Us Pickup's pies,' growled Jurassic Jeff.

'Stew and 'ard,' piped Jimmy Capstick, 'And peas what's already soaked.'

'Blood drinks,' hissed Red Eileen.

'Giblets,' spat Her-from-Next-Door. 'Loose.'

'My Harvest Festivals,' cried Hilda-the-Ton, alluding to the knickers she buys from the knicker stall, large enough to patch the Hindenberg.

For each of us a part of our lives was threatened, which added up left a gaping hole in our existence in the Straggling Town.

'We must fight to the last man and woman,' cried Arthur Wormwell, brandishing a copy of the Ladybird Book of Guerilla Warfare he'd just picked up from the second-hand bookstall.

And Percy Smallcroft slunk away biting his lip to pen a front page article using the words 'mob' and 'ugly scenes' and 'open rebellion.'

Episode 2: Onward Straggling Soldiers

When our MP, the Rt Hon Lester Baggot-Pratt, failed to respond to our letter protesting at the demolition of our market to make way for a Moneygrab Superstore, some direct action was called for. A petition to Parliament was one idea. But we could find no one prepared to go to London. What did we want with such a self-important monstrosity where no one ever spoke and there wasn't a single moortop where you could exercise your whippet? Besides, what had Parliament ever done for us, there not being a single consultancy fee or free foreign holiday to be had from the town? Though it's understood Pickup's Pies once approached Cyril Smith for an endorsement, but could never get close enough.

But Baggot-Pratt, or the Prat, as we preferred to call him, was a different cup of tea – or glass of chablis might be a better way of putting it. He depended on our vote – not that anyone in the Straggling Town would ever admit to voting for him. Many years ago we had been the victims of boundary changes which made about as much sense as a triangular bicycle wheel. We had been tagged on to a leafy shire to the north, a well-shod dale of purple-faced majors and jodphur-clad Jocasters; where 4-wheel drives with kangaroo bars for maiming dawdling peasants bullied their way along every thoroughfare, and vowels were as long and drawn out as their bank balances. The voters there had as much in common with us in the Straggling Town as Christine Hamilton has with Mother Teresa.

We decided on a protest march to the Prat's country seat. Or an Unholy Crusade, as Arthur Wormwell put it.

Echoes of the Jarrow March were there, but only dimly. None of us was hungry. It was about twelve miles over the moors to Pratt Manor, and Fred Pickup had put an extra shift on at the pie factory to sustain us on our way. Her-from-the-Tripe-Stall had ordered an extra gross of black puddings, and there were enough buttered Eccles cakes to tile the Space Shuttle. Braithwaites Brewery had gener-  ously brewed and bottled a unique ale for the occasion. It was called Old Tosser, though any suggestion that the name was inspired by our MP himself would be strenu- ously denied by their solicitors. Several crates had been strategically placed at various staging posts on the journey – about every half-mile.

The day of the march dawned bright and warm. We'd decided to convene at the Poet and Peasant Working Men's Club where a breakfast of bacon barm cakes set us up for the journey. It was also decided that a crate or two of Old Tosser should be breached to fortify the spirits for what could be a dangerous campaign. 'Salient' Sam Wilkinson, our only surviving World War One veteran, likened it to the tots of rum issued to the men going over the top. It was indeed hostile territory we were

venturing into. Already the smell of Chanel perfume and kedgeree was
wafting provocatively towards us on the breeze, mingling strangely with
our own native smell of gas tar and chip fat. Furred arteries began to fizz
and pop with adrenalin. Wives who had to stay at home to donkeystone
the step waved and wept, and babies were held aloft to witness history in
the making as the Straggling Town Prize Band struck up to see us on our
way.

Arthur Wormwell had scoured the attic at the Warp Dressers' Club and
come up with a banner. It once belonged to the Straggling Town branch
of the Union of Burlers and Menders. Pity no one was still around to
practise the craft on the banner itself. The moths had been at it and it
resembled an over-sized string vest. But no matter. It was a symbol of
solidarity, a rallying point like the battle standards of old. Other, home-
made, banners were brandished. 'Save Our Market' was the most popular,
though Bag o' Nails bore one with a skull and crossbone with the chilling
words, 'He is Waiting!', which no one else could fathom.

But despite this, the mood was jolly, with many dressed in traditional
costume. Red Eileen looked particularly comely in a bonnet and shawl, if
you ignored the menacing sash of her scarlett orafice and the razor blades
hidden in her clogs.

The journey passed off without event, apart from the repeated stops on
the way for liquid refreshment. That these were many and prolonged could
be judged by the steady increase in the volume of the singing. What had
begun as an occasional flurry of 'Onward Christian Soldiers' gradually gave
way to rousing choruses of the 'Red Flag'. By the time we had breasted
the hill which overlooked the Dale of Plenty, all birdsong had stopped and
a deathly hush had invaded the shire.

Pratt Manor shone in the afternoon sunlight like a well-greased palm.
A large marquee had been erected upon one of its ample lawns. From its
cool interior came the pop of champagne corks and the tinkle of expensive
crystal. And another sound. One to raise the hackles of every honest,
hard-working Straggling Towner: the concerted purr of fat cats lazily
grooming their pampered fur.

'My dear, you simply must taste the crudités.'

'She's staying with Miles and Caractacus in Belgravia.'

'You still can't beat bricks and mortar for an investment.'

And outside, the sound of teeth being ground together.

But no one moved. Irresolution seized us. What was holding us back?
Was it some age-old habit of subservience in the presence of our 'betters'
that would soon have us reaching for our caps and tugging at our forelocks?

Then the tap of a silver spoon upon bone china.

'Ladies and Gentlemen. Fellow shareholders of Moneygrab,' came the voice of Lester Baggot-Pratt. 'Our Chairman and my dear friend, Hugo Sackbutt.'

(A patter of doughy applause – soft hands that knew not work and had never held a posser or a mangle.)

'Fellow shareholders. It is with the deepest satisfaction that I am able to announce a modest increase in this year's dividend of 93%. Now while I know that none of you would be seen dead in one of our stores, and we certainly don't propose to start stocking caviar on the shelves next to the spam, haw, haw, haw, nevertheless, we are growing ever more popular with the lower and feckless classes. In fact, we are soon to begin work on our hundredth store, not many miles away from here –'

He got no further before the roof fell in. A simultaneous severing of the guy ropes brought the marquee crashing to the ground. Complacent drawls gave way to muffled wails of terror as animated lumps of striped canvas struggled to crawl free. But not before they were fallen upon by Red Eileen and her crew armed with umbrellas, stout handbags and the odd knitting needle, and generally poked, jabbed and beaten like an old coker mat in need of a good spring clean. Those who did manage to wriggle free had to contend with the terrifying sight of Jurassic Jeff standing over them and annointing their heads with the left-overs from several bottles of Old Tosser.

It was a comprehensive victory for the great unwashed, and that night at our own celebratory banquet of a pie and pea supper back at the Poet and Peasant, the spoils of war were on display. These included the surgical truss of a retired Field Marshall and the false teeth of a Dowager Duchess. Our only casualty was Bag o' Nails, who had been bitten by a deportment instructress from Harrogate Ladies' College who he was convinced was rabid. Stacking several pints of Braithwaites bitter before him, none of which he refused, convinced him he had nothing to fear.

Episode 3: A Big Flap Over the Market

Our sabotage of the shareholders' meeting of the Moneygrab supermarket chain did nothing to delay the planned destruction of our market to make room for their latest store. Well-greased wheels moved rapidly within wheels to punish our impudence. The Rt Honourable Lester Baggot-Pratt threatened to take us to court for damaging his marquee, but since the only damage was to the pride of a few pompous plutocrats, he soon dropped the idea. But nightly visits by the police to the Poet and Peasant Club at closing time made sorry inroads into bar takings. But every cloud has a silver lining, and it meant that many of us were home in time to enjoy the rich cultural delights of Prisoner Cell Block H on television. A deputation of food standards officers from the European Union arrived from Brussels at the Pickup Pie factory, insisting upon a standard circumference for all pie crusts. When Fred Pickup said he didn't understand what a circumference was, an official tried to explain that it was pi times diameter. 'But was pie a meat and potato or cheese and onion?' demanded Fred, and they went away to deal with simpler matters like shrimp net sizes. Bag o' Nails reckoned his telephone was being tapped and that GCHQ at Cheltenham had been put on red alert monitoring every telephone conversation in the town for evidence of further planned subversion. What they'd make of our frequent passionate exchanges about the price of wetfish and the suitability of the weather for transplanting brassicas, who will ever know? Perhaps the country's top code-breakers are cudgelling their brains at this very moment. But one thing was for sure. Our MP had sat up and taken notice of us at last. For years all he'd done was to pop up at election time to kiss a few babies before hurrying off home to wash his mouth out with Listerine. Now he knew he had a nest of vipers on his doorstep.

A few of the snakes in question were sunning themselves on the seats outside the library. Arthur Wormwell had been in there to borrow their entire stock of books on guerilla warfare, causing a startled librarian to ring up her boss at County Hall to enquire whether MI5 should be informed.

The books he'd got weren't exactly dynamite. One was a songbook of revolutionary campfire verses translated from the Bolivian and entitled *Sing Along With Ché*. The other was issued in error by a junior assistant and was a handbook on rearing large monkeys by the gorilla keeper from London Zoo. But the important thing was that we'd started to plan our campaign of protest.

Jimmy Capstick has ears like another large zoo animal, and Bag o' Nails suggested taking a leaf out of the book of the airport protestors and nailing one of them to the counter of the tripe stall. Jimmy, whose idea of a martyr is something you put on a ham sandwich, wasn't so keen on the idea and thought supergluing Bag o' Nails' nose – another prominent appendage – to the backside of the statue of Councillor Amos Slack which stands just outside the market, would do just as well. The discussion had begun to degenerate into an exchange of personal insults when we suddenly observed three familiar figures slipping into the market hall by a side door. A flash of copper like a signal fire announced Red Eileen with the Ponderous One and Her-from-Next-Door.

'Now I wonder what they're up to?' said Arthur Wormwell.

The next day, at dawn, the town was abuzz. Here in the Straggling Town we're normally asleep till the streets are aired, or at least until the first batch of Pickup's pies are out of the oven. But today the sun had barely got his hat on before people were ringing one another up or else tossing dried peas at their bedroom windows. We'd been invaded.

We hurried up to the market to find it ringed by a human chain of security men in white safety helmets and yellow jackets with 'Flog 'em and Hang 'em Security Ltd' written on the back. Strutting amongst them like a poodle at Crufts was a pipsqueak in a suit.

'Ladies and Gentlemen,' he announced through a loud hailer. 'You are advised to return to your beds before they cool. Any attempt to interfere with the demolition of this building will be met with arrest according to the powers invested in me as the Under-Sheriff of this County.'

We'd never had a sheriff in town before. Plenty of outlaws and our share of sheep rustlers. But not a sheriff.

'Where's your star, then?' shouted Arthur Wormwell, and the line of security men stiffened like a row of bared yellow teeth.

Then we spotted a familiar figure. He was twice as wide as the others, and even though he'd tried to disguise himself by pulling his helmet down over his eyes, there was no mistaking the neck, like a capstan used to moor the *Ark Royal*.

'Judas Iscariot!' gasped Bag o' Nails. 'It's Jurassic Jeff.' And Jeff went so

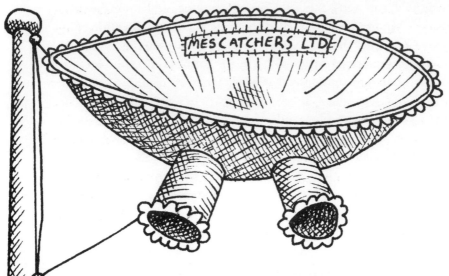

red you could no longer see the drops of blood on the daggers tattooed on his neck.

'Jeffrey,' came a strident voice from the crowd, 'Come out of there, at once,' and a small, snapping, Jack Russell of a woman barged her way to the front and grabbing Jeff by one ear, hauled him away. 'But I needed the money to buy me pies, Mam,' whimpered the sumo wrestler turned doormouse.

'There'll be no pies if the market closes, you lard brain,' cried his mother, and snatching the helmet off his head, threw it at the Under-Sheriff. 'Corrupting my lad,' she snapped. 'You ought to be ashamed. Get back to Nottingham, Sheriff, where you belong.'

Just then the bulldozers arrived, trundling over the cobbles, scoops raised menacingly to tear the heart out of our town. We all froze, like patients under ether.

Then, from the roof a sudden flickering movement. Something began inching its way up the flagpole. Something large and sugarbag blue. And when it reached the top it stretched itself like some headless torso and it began to flap with the sharp, cracking sound of stiffened sailcloth.

'Hilda-the-Ton's knickers,' cried Her-from-the-Knicker-Stall. 'I'd recognise those anywhere.' Handsewn by the same company who make windsocks for Squire's Gate airport. 'Hilda's in there. Stop the machines!'

The Sheriff, red with fury, began barking into his mobile phone. The machines ground to a standstill. 'By 'eck,' cried one of the drivers appreciatively. 'That must be a grand, big woman.'

Then, to a giant roar from the crowd, out they came onto the roof.

Hilda, Eileen and Her-from-Next-Door. They proceeded to chain themselves to the flagpole before the arrival of a fourth stalwart, Doris from the Cosy Cafe, who bore a tray full of her freshly made rag puddings, steaming in a sea of piping marrowfat peas and ox-tail gravy. 'Cheers,' shouted Eileen, and they began digging in with a will.

Knowing he was beaten, the Sheriff ordered a strategic withdrawal. The crowd cheered again, the rooftop heroines waved their spoons and the big blue knickers flapped proudly in the breeze that whipped round the corner of Woolworths.

We retired to command headquarters – the Poet and Peasant – to discuss the next phase of our campaign. But most of our time was spent discussing where to put Hilda's bloomers on the coat-of-arms we were designing for the newly independent Straggling Town.

Episode 4: Staggering Developments

As it became clear that the powers that be were hell bent on the demolition of our market, only one course remained open to us. We must declare the Straggling Town independent. No more playing second fiddle to the suited bully-boys of Graythorpe and Witherslack. From now on we'd run the town the way we wanted it.

There was an air of nervous excitement in the Poet and Peasant Working Men's Club as we sat down to discuss our next move.

'No good will come of it,' forecast Bag o' Nails, staring moodily into his empty glass and hoping that someone would take pity on him. 'It's treason. They can still hang you by the neck for it till your eyes pop out.' And he leant forward, warming to his theme. 'That's why they put a mask over their heads, so you can't see the horrible things it does to them.' And he made a face like a constipated gargoyle, so that Fred Dobson, who's bad with his nerves, flinched so violently he spilt his beer.

'Oh shut up, for goodness sake,' cried Arthur Wormwell. 'You sound like a guide at Madam Tussauds. Now, I've been thinking,' he went on, 'what's the first thing they do in these third world countries when they declare independence?'

'Start looting?' cried Jimmy Capstick eagerly. He'd had his eyes on a hi-fi system in Rumbelow's for some time now.

'Rape?' said Fred Chadwick, who'd long had a secret admiration for Hilda-the-Ton's Himalayan frontage.

Arthur ignored them. 'I'll tell you what they do. They take over the nearest radio station and broadcast their intentions to the world.'

But who was going to write down our manifesto? Percy Smallcroft was our most gifted wordsmith. His reports of the Golden Cue Snooker Competition had been known to bring tears to the eyes of lovers of the Queen's English. But since we'd accused him of being on the side of the supermarket developers and snapped all his ballpoints, he'd been sulking in the Pack o' Lies. And who would do the reading? Bag o' Nails' tone was so melancholy he'd been known to set all the dogs off howling in Balaclava Street. Fred Dobson stammered if he got worked up. If we brought Red Eileen in she'd hector the audience to death. We finally settled on Arthur Wormwell's cousin, Eric. He was rather dull. In fact, he had about as much appeal as a weekend winter break in Morecambe. But he had experience of global communications. He was a radio ham, and sat up every night having long conversations about foot rot and liver fluke with Australian sheep-shearers. He could be the new Chris Evans.

But how do you take over a radio station? At gunpoint? The only person we knew with a gun was Reuben Moorhead, but the way he lets fly at all and sundry who wander onto his farmland, we'd end up with a massacre on our hands.

'We go to the studios to be interviewed for something else,' said Fred Chadwick, the butcher. 'Once inside we can take over.'

Fred was no stranger to media fame. He'd once taken part in a Mad Cow Special, a studio debate chaired by local radio star Guy Maverick, real name Cyril Booth, three times winner of the Sony Silver Tongue Award, a man whose unctuous charms oozed out of our radio sets like rancid butter. Invited to speak on the safety of British beef, Fred had startled the studio guests by consuming a whole string of his own beef chipolatas raw before their very eyes. It didn't do his argument much good as most sensible people saw this as evidence of advanced brain decay and peanut burgers were on everybody's shopping list for ages.

Another barrel of Braithwaites bitter was drawn as our own brains were stretched for a good reason to appear on his show. Bag o' Nails, with an astute eye for the public interest in medical matters, suggested taking in his collection of diseased organs which he'd bought off a hard-up medical student for five pounds. He'd once given a talk on a wet Tuesday at the club when the darts match was cancelled. The sight of all those moribund gall bladders and stricken livers lying in bottles of brown formalin put everyone off their beer, and for the first time in its history the bar was closed by nine-thirty. Arthur Wormwell was an acknowledged expert on World War II gas masks and could wax quite lyrically on the use of the khaki bags for carrying trainspotting equipment. And there was our gardening expert, Ernest Fothergill, who could talk for hours on wireworms. Which is not as dull as it sounds as he reaches surprising metaphysical heights. The wireworm, he reckons, is conclusive proof that God does not exist, because no one in their right mind could create such a pointless little horticultural vandal. But we finally decided on something of more main-stream interest and hit on the idea of posing as the Straggling Town branch of the Alma Cogan Appreciation Society, eager to drum up support for a charity night of Fifties Fun at the Pack o' Lies.

Humming 'I saw Mommy Kissing Santa Claus Underneath the Christmas Tree Last Night', because it was the only Alma Cogan song any of us could remember, we were shown into the studio. Suddenly we all began to feel nervous. Arthur Wormwell, a bit of a bar stool psychologist, correctly identified this as the Yapping Dog Syndrome. The smallest dog will go for your heels in its own backyard, further afield it becomes an abject coward. We felt the same. Away from the cosy familiarity of the Straggling Town, surrounded by self-assured young men in button-down shirts, clutching clipboards and dictating the latest news from Moscow and the high tides at Fleetwood to secretaries cool as ice, we began to feel out of our depth. How dare we expect the big wide world to take any notice of us and our petty concerns?

But it was too late to turn back. Guy Maverick had begun his introduc-tion and we were stuck, like flies in molasses.

'... a warm welcome to the members of the *Staggering* Town Alma Cogan Appreciation Society.'

For those listeners with a keen ear and VHF, the sound of mouths opening and shutting like asphixiating fish was audible.

'Alma,' went on the great man, like warm vaseline, 'a lovely, bubbly girl. I knew her personally of course.' Perhaps he wouldn't need us after all. 'Such warmth. Such vibrance. Such *joie de vivre*. We in the business loved her dearly. I remember the time ...'

'Straggling,' boomed Bag o' nails, like the siren on the *Titanic*. 'It's the Straggling Town, not Staggering.'

'Huh,' said Guy Maverick, positively peevish that anyone should interrupt his flow. 'Straggling, staggering, what's the difference between friends?'

And suddenly, Jurassic Jeff showed him with a friendly push that sent him staggering off his chair and across the studio.

Our confidence wonderfully restored, Eric grabbed the microphone and we announced our independence from the rest of the world.

The broadcast was a staggering success. People rang in offering blankets and tins of baked beans. A firm donated a thousand boxes of cotton buds.

We got a letter of support from Dennis Skinner and the Tockholes Branch of the Free East Timor Society. Several veterans from Greenham Common phoned in with instructions on how to build tepees, and collections of morale boosting fireside songs. We'd got our message across. We were ready for the great siege. Tomorrow the barricades would go up. Long Live the People's Republic of the Staggering – er, Straggling – Town!

Episode 5: Manning, and Womanning, the Barricades

Only one road leads into the Straggling Town. It winds and weaves its way along the straggling valley, climbing all the time, and in the process it succeeds in losing most people. The river passes it on the way, hurrying in the opposite direction. As it swirls and bubbles over the stones it seems to whisper: 'I don't know why you're going there. There's nowt there but a lot of queer folk. I'm off to somewhere more interesting.' And it rushes off to the seaside like an excited Wakes Week holidaymaker.

Now this one approach road means that the Straggling Town is very easy to defend. We can look down the valley and see who's coming long before they've decided whether they're going to bother or not. Now during the last war they took advantage of our unique position to defend us from the jackboots of the deranged Austrian Adolf. A concrete pillbox still stands by the roadside. It's a scene of happy reminiscences for some of the older end of Straggling Towners like Jack Robinson and Ernest Fothergill, who spent many nights in there with the Home Guard, a Woodbine and hipflask to their lips, ready to repulse the Hun with one Lee Enfield rifle between six of them. Long has the pillbox remained in disuse, its narrow peepholes blocked with weeds, its black insides stuffed with binbags full of rubbish and its clay floor scattered with empty cider bottles and the cold remains of campfires lit by tramps and refugees from civilisation and Noel Edmond's House Party.

But not tonight. Anyone foolish enough to pass that way – without knowing the secret password, 'Pickup's pies are best!' – would have observed a flickering light through the peepholes and the smell of woodsmoke. They would have heard the murmur of eager conversation and the merry fizz of bottle tops being released. And if they'd eluded the ever-vigilant eye of the lookout, fast asleep in the warm moonlight on top of the pillbox, they'd have found inside as stout a band of heroes, ready to defend their liberties to the last drop of Braithwaite's bitter, as ever lived and ate an Eccles cake.

The campfire danced in their eyes, rekindling flames that hadn't burnt so bright for forty years, not since the First Straggling Town Mayor's Own

Wolf Cubs had their annual camps at the Water Meetings and Akala used to sit them round the fire and tell them ghost stories. The floor was strewn with sleeping bags. It had been swept clean and scattered with fresh straw from Reuben Moorhead's barn.

'It beats sitting at home watching the telly,' said Jimmy Capstick, poking at the fire to check on how the baked potatoes were doing.

'Mind you don't set fire to any of that straw,' warned Bag o' Nails, 'else we'll all roast to death like spuds in their jackets.'

As usual, his was the one note of discord in a happy camp. We'd had an excellent day. We'd turned back several enemy vehicles. Most of them had been spies from the Graythorpe and Witherslack District Council, claiming we were interfering with essential Council services by not letting them past. Arthur Wormwell had politely pointed out that we'd already been waiting for a year for them to replace the glass in the bus shelter outside the library, so another year or two standing getting soaked in the rain wasn't going to matter. And if it was the street lamps on Mizpah Street that came on during the day and went out at night, well they'd been like that for so long we'd got used to them and we all slept much better in the dark. And if they were talking about mowing the grass verges, we'd rather do it ourselves than wait until it poured down like the Council before they sent someone to churn it into a mudbath. Everyone knew what they really wanted: to come and knock down our last remaining public asset, the market, and hand it over to the bandits from Moneygrab.

The police had left us alone – like they do until after a crime's committed. After all, we hadn't done anything wrong yet. It was a peaceful picket. The road was free for traffic to pass. It was just that if they didn't look like stopping, Hilda-the-Ton suddenly appeared in the road like a Sherman tank. And with Red Eileen and Her-from-Next-Door soon at her side, no man or woman born dare proceed without permission.

Which brings us to the matter of where the gentler sex were at that moment. Imbued with a deep mistrust of menfolk, to say nothing of an unconfirmed sighting of a *News of the World* reporter on the lookout for a Rude Romps in Roadside Pillbox story, a strict segregation of the sexes had been observed. Red Eileen and her henchwomen were at that moment comfortably bivouacked in a bright orange tent at the opposite side of the road, with a spacious flysheet extension to house Hilda, who had been unable to fit into the main body of the tent.

We were not, however, isolated. Arthur Wormwell's cousin, Eric, our electronics wizard, had installed a telephone link between the two camps, and unbeknown to the rest of us, Fred Chadwick, the butcher, who harboured a secret passion for the ample flanks and stupendous udders of Hilda, had sneaked into a darkened corner of the pillbox and at that moment was whispering sweet endearments into it in the hope that the object of his passion might be at hand to respond.

'Je t'aime, ma petite,' he croaked, in a creditable French accent acquired from visiting black pudding conventions in France, which, unknown to Mrs Chadwick, always seemed to be held in the red light district of Paris.

Suddenly a shrill whistle blasted back over the telephone. This was one of Red Eileen's remedies for telephone heavy-breathers. It shook us out of our sense of complacency. It also awoke our look-out on the roof, just in time for him to spot a convoy of wagons winding their way up the valley road.

He burst into the pillbox like an opening shot at snooker.

'They're here,' he gasped. 'The army's coming.'

We dashed outside. He was right. They were army wagons, their canvas roofs plainly visible in the moonlight. An armoured car and jeep headed the procession.

'I told you we should never have started this,' whispered Bag o' Nails, displaying the true bulldog spirit and falling to his knees.

'I'm off,' shouted Jimmy Capstick, heading for the open moor.

'Shoot all deserters,' shrieked Red Eileen, stopping him in his tracks.

We all moved into the road, hearts in our mouths. Armchair anarchists no more, this was the real thing. We were up against the armed might of the Establishment now. Would we crumble? Would our children live to renounce us as craven capitulators? Cowards and funks? The roar of the wagons drowned the sound of the blood in our ears.

Then the jeep stopped and a young officer jumped out, bristling like a yardbrush.

'Is this Holcombe Moor?' he asked, winking appreciatively at Hilda-the-Ton. 'T.A. manoeuvres, old bean, ye know.'

'No, you're miles away,' said Arthur Wormwell, pointing back down the valley. 'Back where you came.'

'By the way,' he said, before getting back into the jeep, gazing mystified at the odd assortment of townspeople. 'What are you doing out at this time?'

'Same as you,' said Arthur. 'Making sure the rest can sleep easily in their beds.'

The officer clicked his well-polished heels together. 'Damned good show. Keep up the good work,' and turning his convoy round, they left.

There was a universal sigh of relief. Or it could have been the sound of many bottles being opened to steady the nerves.

Episode 6: Parlous Goings-on

Arthur Wormwell's eyes shone with inspiration. It was the evening after our declaration of independence from the jackboot of the Graythorpe and Witherslack District Council. The Straggling Town was free. We would keep our market and the Mongeygrab Superstore could take its bandywheeled trolleys and donkey burgers somewhere else. The infant true democracy was born, turned upside down and smacked firmly on the bottom before issuing its first lusty cry. And Arthur Wormwell saw all this and his eyes sparkled.

Of course, others at the bar of the Poet and Peasant Working Men's Club with their feet more to the ground, saw only the effects of the second pint of Old Rapture strong ale which Arthur at that moment was raising to his lips before lowering with a smacking sound like a family of molluscs detaching themselves from Duncan Goodhew's head. There is always a moment about half-way through the second pint of Old Rapture when the universe, with all its maddening frustrations, suddenly slips quietly into place and a state of supreme wellbeing invades the spirits of the imbiber. Usually nothing can destroy this sense of bliss – apart from the calling of last orders, but since it was only half-past seven, and the night itself was still only an infant, there was no danger of that.

'We will be an example to the nation,' sighed Arthur beatifically. 'Nay, to the world. Democrats and libertarians will come from far and wide to see true democracy at work. A town run by the people for the people.' He took another mouthful of the sublime nectar. 'Like Tolpuddle, the Straggling Town has entered the history books.'

The briefest hint at martyrdom brought our Prophet of Doom out of his corner like Mother Shipton out of her cave.

'Aye,' said Bag o' Nails, 'the only thing that'll get us into the history books will be an outbreak of the plague. There's folk complaining already that they haven't had their dustbins emptied. How long before we're opening our back doors to rats the size of tom cats?'

'There's no chance of that,' replied Jimmy Capstick. 'Reuben Moorhead'd been round with his tractor. For a pound he's taking people's bin bags and emptying 'em in Fiddler's Clough.'

'And Horace Fenwick's running the library,' said Fred Chadwick the butcher. 'They say he's replaced *The Times* and *People's Friend* in the reading room with *The Sunday Sport* and *Health and Efficiency*. There's a queue for them half way down the street.'

Arthur Wormwell groaned and put down his glass, his dreams in tatters.

'Anarchy. That's just what our enemies want to see. What we need is some organisation. We must call a meeting in the Town Hall.'

Now our Town Hall has been mothballed since the District Council took over. They'd had plans to turn it into a rifle range for one-armed Lesbians until someone from the Civic Society pointed out that riccochets might damage the historic plasterwork. So it had been locked up pending some further hare-brained proposal by the enlightened human beings who brought us line-dancing on the rates and tried to twin us with Auschwitz. But could we persuade the caretaker to open it? Norman Ratcliff was devoted to his calling of polishing parquet floors and brassoing doorknobs. He's learnt his trade from his father who had been in charge at Corunna Road Junior and Infants Mixed when we'd all been there over 40 years ago. There'd been nothing quite like the self-important swagger he'd put on as he sallied forth with the firebucket full

of sawdust when someone was sick on the hall floor during assembly. And he used to report us to the headmaster for weeing over the wall of the boys' lavatory into the big girls' playground: something boys of nine have got to do to prove their manhood and requires a painful amount of squeezing. But would Norman relinquish his jealous guardianship of the Town Hall? It was rumoured he slept in the mayor's parlour and strutted about in his regalia. And he was definitely odd. Anyone who disturbed him might expect the same reception as from his namesake, Norman Bates, and get the shower-curtain treatment. Nevertheless, fearless revolutionaries that we were, we decided to pay him a visit, there and then.

It isn't often you find yourself agreeing with the Victorians, but they had the right idea as far as our towns were concerned. There was no sharing for them, no such thing as rationalisation to save a few bob and put it in the pockets of a bloated Chief Executive and his cronies, and all at the expense of civic pride. Every town had its own town hall, its own bit of grandeur to lift the spirits of the work-worn; for them to stand and look up, push back their caps and say, 'By gum, but that's grand! And it's ours!' Now, as the setting sun sank over Blackedge Reservoir, the soft coppery

rays brought a warm flush of pride to the millstone grit. There were carved
scrolls and lions rampant, mythical beasts with bulging eyes and tongues
that lolled like ours before opening time. Funny how you never notice
things until they're taken away from you, but our town hall was a work
of art. Now it was ours again. We were laying claim to it like a long lost
inheritance.

But getting inside was another matter. Arthur Wormwell winced as his
knuckles met the huge oak door. His knocks rang hollow inside the
cavernous interior. Outside, the main street was quiet. It was eyes down
at Lucky Numbers Bingo and the Chinese chippy was deserted, and would
stay that way until closing time when hunger strikes like a cobra, and only
chips embalmed in curry sauce, and stuff to turn a sober stomach inside
out, will satisfy the craving. We stood on the great stone steps as the town
hall clock struck eight and the pigeons nudged and shuffled their way to
bed on the high stone ledges above our heads.

'There's no one here,' growled Bag o' Nails. 'Let's get back to t' club
before they sup the rest of t' Old Rapture.'

But just then the brass flap of the huge letter-box inched back and a
voice hissed out, 'Clear off, you kids. I've told you before.'

'Norman?' whispered Arthur Wormwell. 'Can you let us in?'

A pair of shifty eyes, swollen with mistrust, peered through the letter
box.

'No one's allowed in 'ere,' said Norman. 'Orders of the Council.'

'There is no Council now. It's us,' said Arthur Wormwell. 'It's our town
hall now. It belongs to the Straggling Town.'

A long pause while Norman's brain, which no amount of Brasso could
brighten digested this fact. 'I'm only doing my job,' he replied, the official
local government response to a difficult situation.

Jimmy Capstick tried another tack. 'We know what you're wearing,' he
sang. 'Do you want us to tell them at Graythorpe about it?'

There was a feverish rustling sound and the unmistakable chink of a
heavy chain being removed, not from the door but from around Norman's
neck. Then there was the grate of a key being turned in the huge lock.

As the door opened, Norman stood there sheepishly. He'd forgotten to
remove the mayor's three-cornered hat, and in his khaki overall he looked
like a down-at-heel rear admiral.

'Now, show us the council chamber, Norman,' ordered Arthur Wormwell, 'and you can get back to the parlour and your fancy dress parade.'

We stood under the crystal chandeliers, gawping up at the coloured
ceiling with all the coats of arms of famous Straggling Town families. Stern

aldermen glared back at us from sepia portraits, outraged at the invasion. 'All ours, lads,' whispered Arthur Wormwell.

'Not on your nelly!' screeched a voice like a chain-saw, and Red Eileen and her crew burst in like harpies. 'Men are not running this town no more. It's our turn.' And the stern faces of the onlooking aldermen blanched like almonds.

We did the only thing that proud, courageous and sensible men could do in such a situation: we beat a hasty retreat back to our bar stools at the Poet and Peasant. There was a lot we had to learn about popular revolutions, not least that they were followed by power struggles and nights of long knives.

Meanwhile, it may have been observed by those leaving the Lucky Numbers Bingo Club later that night that rouched pink curtains were going up at the windows of the town hall. Crocheted antimacassars found their way over all the chairs, and Norman Ratcliff was encouraged to swap his overall for a floral pinafore with a headscarf and feather duster. Which we think he rather enjoyed.

Episode 7: A Shining Example

It was no surprise when the womenfolk took over the running of the Straggling Town. They've always been our mainstay: running the house and six looms, disappearing for a day or two to have babies, then back into harness. While the men sit around in the pub or club, self-importantly putting the world to right or pontificating about cars and football. It happens in tribes the world over: the men huff and puff and emptily rattle their spears, while the women pound away at the grindstone, keep the fire going, balance babies on their backs and give suck, all at the same time.

But it wasn't long before, here in the Straggling Town, they abandoned the Town Hall. After putting scalloped lace vallances round all the desks and a Laura Ashley floral canopy over the mayor's chair, they decided the council chamber still wasn't comfy enough. So they moved to the Cosy Cafe on the Market, and that triumvirago whom no man durst disobey – Red Eileen, Hilda-the-Ton, and Her-from-Next-Door – set up their administrative headquarters. Here at the red formica table, with a squidgy plastic tomato and crusty brown sauce bottle replacing the civic mace, over gallons of tea, brown as the river Wharfe in spate, and buttered Eccles

cakes bearing the thumb-print of the waitress, the affairs of the Straggling Town were conducted with all the smoothness of a greased pig slipping through the bare arms of a drunken bumpkin. Not a dull-eyed local government official to be seen. Not a computer, fax machine, fancy logo or stale promise about service to the community instead of themselves, anywhere. No pompous committees headed by people calling themselves after furniture. No claptrap picked up from drunken seminars on the rates at Clacton-on-Sea. No political correctness humbug. Just: 'Nar then. Sit yourself down. Have a cuppa tea. What's up?' And it all got sorted out in less time than it takes to count the noughts in a Chief Executive's salary. And Doris's cafe didn't half go a bomb. Business was so good she could afford to provide meals-on-wheels to everyone who needed them for nothing. No one slipped through the net, not in a town where minding someone else's business comes before minding your own. Bag o' Nails had no sooner barricaded himself into his cellar in a home-made Andersen shelter because he'd just watched a programme about the dangers of asteroids hitting the earth, when someone was pushing steak and kidney pudding and treacle sponge through his coal-hole to make sure he didn't starve.

There wasn't a service that had been run by the council that Eileen and Hilda and the girls couldn't organise better over a cup of Yorkshire tea and a slice of parkin. Even road traffic mismanagement. No need for any more traffic calming measures to reduce the highway to a crazy golf course of ramps and roundabouts and creeping red tarmac patches that no one can fathom the reason for. Just Jurassic Jeff at the curb side flexing his tatoos and gnawing a ham shank, and Jimmy Capstick, who's always dreamt of driving a big red bus, running a free service to and from the most popular destinations, like the bingo club and the cemetery. True, the Old Pals Memorial Park got a bit overgrown and taking your dog for a walk was like going on safari. But then Reuben Moorhead had the idea of grazing his sheep on it. We think it gives a more natural, rural look, much better than park rangers driving around in body armour with stun guns, pistol-whipping kids they catch fishing for tadpoles in the frog pond. Some of the fussier off-comed-uns from the new estate complained that they got sheep-droppings stuck to their pants when they knelt to bowl on the bowling green. But the general feeling is that people who wear white flannels to bowl shouldn't be in the Straggling Town but should go and live somewhere posh like Lytham St Annes in a beige brick bungalow.

The spectacle of Red Eileen and Hilda and Her-from-Next-Door convened in the Cosy Cafe did a lot to improve behaviour in the town. Parents whose children never went anywhere without their social worker now only had to bring them into the Market, where the sight of the three sisters was enough to make them vow to do missionary work for the rest of their lives. Eileen, now that she was in the public eye so much, had started to henna dye her hair at least three times a week. It bore all the appearance of a raging bonfire. The livid slash of her lipsticked mouth and getting a painter and decorator in to rouge her cheeks, made her look like the demon harlot from Hell. And if that alone wasn't enough to strike terror into the soul of the God-fearing, there was Hilda-the-Ton looking like Moby Dick. The continual presence of so much temptation in the shape of Doris's vanilla slices, chocolate eclairs and an irresistible confection known as suffocation by syrup, had crowded yet more inches to Hilda's stupendous girth. Only the introduction of a concrete litter bin beneath her chair prevented its collapse. And, Her-from-Next-Door, while small, packed all the venom of an Australian funnel web spider. Add to this terrifying trio the insidious network of gossip inspired by a town run by women, and the fear of being at the centre of it, and you have the best recipe for moral improvement since the Ten Commandments. In fact, to the astonishment of the outside world, the Straggling Town disappeared completely from the country's table of crime statistics, the only recorded misdemeanours being the wanton destruction of all signs bearing the insignia of the Graythorpe and Witherslack District Council and the decapitation of the statue of Alderman Amos Slack, whose grandson Horace was leader of the Council and who had wanted to knock down our market in the first place. So impressed was the rest of the world by the harmony and efficiency with which we ran our own affairs, that professors and important people who spend their time in think tanks – whom Jimmy Capstick took to be some sort of human gold fish – asked permission to come to the town to study us. We became the subject of learned papers delivered to academic gatherings, and it was nothing to find Japanese television cameras zooming in on the black pudding stall or Eileen wagging a crimson fingernail at a reporter from NBC News. Austin Perry, our Leisure and Tourism Officer was, of course, given his marching orders and invited to take a tour himself of the crocodile swamps of Botswana. His brainchild, the Mother Moleseed Witches Heritage Trail, was no longer needed to draw in the day-trippers: a visit to the Cosy Cafe was enough to satisfy the appetites of the most superstitious believers in witchcraft. The revenue from tourism meant that many a fat wallet was seen at the bar of the Pack o' Lies pub, where Percy Smallcroft, one time reporter for the *Straggling Town Examiner*, sits like a broken Biro. For what is a newspaper reporter with no crime or unhappiness to report?

Sceptics amongst you may wonder, given the huge budgets local governments squander on running towns – fat expenses for councillors and extortionate early-retirement packages for officials – how we managed without their money. Well, due to all the publicity about the way we ran our town, without a single management consultant, public relations department or army of soft-palmed graduates in Business Administration recruited from Board Schools recently upgraded to universities, word got to Brussels that we were some poor peasant economy, on a par with a bandit-torn village in Sicily or a remote Greek island still ravaged by gangs of blind Cyclopses. As a result, European money came pouring in by every post. Doris was able to install silver candelabras next to the sauce bottles in the Cosy Cafe and we got World of Leather to fit us out with new bar furniture at the Poet and Peasant.

As we sat there, daintily nibbling the crust of a Pickup's pie and sucking the froth off our pints of Old Rapture, we raised our glasses to the Moneygrab Supermarket chain. Without their greed and scheme to knock down our market and swamp us with slimy ham and pallid own-brand baked beans, we might never have had our revolution and declared our independence. Now, we'd heard that other enlightened towns throughout the land were to follow suit and send big businesses packing in favour of the home-grown. We'd become an example to the world, shining like a tray of fresh tripe.

'Never forget,' said Arthur Wormwell. 'Small is beautiful'. And Jimmy Capstick, who is only four feet ten in his socks, believing this to be a reference to him, blushed to the soles of his elevator shoes and couldn't stop grinning for a whole week.

Chapter Thirty-One

Upon the Midnight Clear

$\mathcal{F}$AR down the valley the sun sank. A fat, red hollyberry dropped into the ice blue waters of the sky. Overhead the light thickened and needles of starfire pricked through. The hills, blacker than black against the petering sky, crouched and gathered themselves to spring. And the narrow valley, sensing the attack of night and a frost to crack iron, drew herself together like a mother hen gathering her chicks under her warm wing.

The sodium lights flickered to life on the main road, a sudden necklace of pomegranate seeds. Someone switched on the floodlights round the church and the ancient, mellow sandstone shone like butter. The Christmas tree outside the library burst into a dizzying display of colour. Science, human ingenuity and seasonal gaiety combined to repel the ancient forces of darkness before they could begin to muster a threat.

And the heart of the town, which was the old open market at the top of the hill, quickened its beat with an urgent sense of expectation.

Fred Chadwick the butcher stood like a sheik in his harem of flesh. Goosepimpled turkeys hung from the roof festooned with chipolata trimmings, while all around shone scoured and glistening pork skin. He was a red meat man himself, through to the marrowbone, and it showed in his florid face and his breath hot as rum punch. He had a sprig of mistletoe in the band of his white hat so that he could lean forward and bestow a seasonal kiss on all his female customers. 'Don't forget the stuffing,' he chortled, handing over the long bags of forcemeat, almost ready to burst at his own merriment.

Across the aisle, Her-from-the-Tripe-Stall was doing a surprisingly brisk trade for Christmas Eve. For the older end in the Straggling Town, luxury was a welcome but unfamiliar guest. Good times had always come with an eye cocked over the shoulder for the hardships on their heels. It was a condition of life in the mills, where recession had followed boom as sure as night followed day. And, like the whalebone they still sold on the knicker stall, there was a strong vein of rectitude which said that all this self-indulgence couldn't be good. An asceticism born of fun-rationed Sundays as a child spent under finger-wagging pulpits in sunless Methodist chapels. So a nice bit of tripe sozzled in vinegar with a slice or two of plain bread and butter would do nicely for a Christmas tea, and the turkey could be put aside and made to do for the rest of the week.

But there was no such frugality abroad on the fruit stall. Drifts of colour and smells almost drowned the senses. Nectarines that shone like summer marigolds, apples whose blushes would shame a rose. Pears and peaches nestling in tissue paper like fragile Christmas baubles. But it was the exotic stuff, which confounded the very notion of the seasons, that drew the eye. Miniature punnets of red currants, strawberries and raspberries to stir dim memories of insect-loud summers and stained and sticky fingers. But these had ripened under some foreign sun, or for all we knew under glass or inside some stainless tank of chemicals, and had been flown in along with their sky-high prices. Strange to see them mingling with our homegrown fare, the chocolate-coloured Ormskirks clad in honest local soil, the sprouts still sweating out the frost, the humble swedes. Matrons who could remember childhood stockings with an orange, nuts and one new penny and a pair of knitted mittons gasped at the profligacy. And Jack Stansfield, who every Christmas morning got up early and went to his allotment to pick his own sprouts, scowled and muttered, 'Wicked.'

Jack was old and his head was full of the past. Ghosts haunted his waking dreams. For him, cobbled streets still rang to the steel bark of clogs and it rained black rain from a sulphurous sky. Giant chimneys still loomed, totems to a heartless god of almost ceaseless production. And the valley sang to the mad music of a hundred-thousand looms. For these valleys were taken over in a way we can't conceive today, to a monstrous obsession. They wove cotton for the world. Saris for Indian princesses, shrouds for Eskimos. Valleys untouched and good for nothing since the groan and shriek of glaciers, became the engine room of Empire. Noisy, dirty, smelly, infinitely congested conduits of toiling humanity from which wealth poured like sap from dark roots. And it made thousands rich who didn't know or even care of our whereabouts. Jack remembered the Christmas Eves then.

The short day draining out of the sky through the rain-smeared panes of the northern lights. But you'd hardly notice because it was winter and the gaslights had been on for most of the afternoon, spilling their yellow light and their smell of empty railway platforms. And suddenly the swing-doors stirred at the far end of the shed and the boss was there. Fobchain girdling his fat waistcoat, an affectation of geniality on his graveyard features fit to crack a cast-iron kettle. They could switch off early. No pay, mind!

He couldn't do with them thinking he'd fallen soft. And it was the signal
for Christmas to begin. A sudden release of steam from the valves in the
great engine house. But they'd need to hurry. Just two days before the
treadmill started up again. Two days before the shuttles snatched the
precious thread of your life and sent it hurtling on again towards eternity.
Hurry! Hurry!

The girls took homemade streamers from their bags and draped them
over their looms. Fancy cakes appeared from nowhere, a piece of homemade
fruit loaf. Even a bottle of elderflower wine which still bore the smell of
summer hedgerows. But only if the boss wasn't looking. Otherwise it would
be instant dismissal. So pop it into my enamel mug and he'll think it's
tea. It was all done in a moment, like a charm. A sudden, impromptu
transformation of that dusty, noisy prison into a carnival. Like butterflies
they took off their headscarves and shook down their hair, dabbed on some
lipstick and began to sing carols. And Jack, with a sprig of mistletoe in his
hand and his heart in his mouth, approached the girl with auburn hair
and sparkling eyes for a brush on the cheek he would remember all his
life.

Back on the market, the girls of yesterday, grown stout or brittle-thin
as china, sat at the cafe drinking tea and eating buttered Eccles cakes. How
had they time on the very brink of Christmas? Well, there was always time
for a good natter, especially if it was seasoned with the spice of scandal.
Red Eileen, her scarlet bouffant specially dyed for Christmas and held in
place under her green headscarf with the scaffolding of two dozen plastic
curlers, sat with the megalithic Hilda-the-Ton. Hilda, to enjoy a guilt-free
Christmas, had been slimming for the past three months. Alas, it was
impossible to tell. Her obstinate body, fearing it was under seige, had stored
every morsel it had been given, converting every last ounce into sebacious
lard, enough to cook the whole town's turkeys and still leave some over
for the roast potatoes. Next to her was Her-from-Next-Door, a mouse of
a thing with a bite that carried rabies. They were discussing Eileen's
neighbour in Disraeli Street who only that morning had flown out to
Lanzarote.

'Sun or no sun,' said Hilda, shaking a dozen chins, 'I couldn't spend
Christmas away from home. Paella instead of mince pies! It doesn't seem
natural.'

Eileen shook her head and the bouffant yawned dangerously. 'That's not
the point. She's gone without her husband. I saw him buying mince in
the Co-op.'

The market stalls were beginning to pack up. The sparrows were ready for their Christmas feast, swooping down to pick up the bits of icing sugar and marzipan from the cake stall. Father Christmas, who'd taken a stall at the end and converted it into a cardboard grotto with a plastic shower curtain over the entrance, wearily lifted his red-flannel sleeve to inspect his wrist-watch again. He'd swallowed so much fluff from his cottonwool beard he had a fireman's thirst upon him. But there were still a dozen children queuing and his seasonal cheer was stretched as tight as the elastic round the back of his head. He feigned to make a note of the umpteenth request for the latest Nintendo and handed over a plastic raygun which he prayed wouldn't break before they left the market. What did they expect for a pound? A glass of beer welled up inside his brain so large that if it had burst it would have flooded the whole valley.

In the place of his day-long thoughts they'd been busy since noon. The bar of the Poet and Peasant Working Men's Club was awash with beery good cheer. Like impatient children eager to get their hands on their presents, the regulars had insisted that the special barrel of Old Rapture being saved for the evening session be drawn there and then. The brewery had hinted at some mysterious ingredient for the festive season, something to improve the brew's already sublime qualities. It had seemed impossible. But if Christmas isn't the time for miracles, when is? Lips could be heard smacking half-a-mile away. Glasses were raised, not just in jolly salutation, but merely to marvel. To glimpse the world through that rich refulgence, that ruby red clarity which is as stained glass to the churchman, and to sigh with as much content as earthly pleasures can bring. Folly? Weakness? Who are we to judge, except to say that these men were middle-aged, farmers who'd scraped a living from our bare hills, miners and weavers whose working lives had been cut short by redundancy. They'd seen their share of hardship, suffering, illness and strife, so if they reached their quietus through a glass, so what? Good luck to them, and cheers!

It was dark now outside. To the slow ratchet of the stars the frost tightened its grip. The streetlights shivered, clasped hands and danced down the valley. They followed the road and the river out of the black hills towards the great plain beyond and the unholy glow of the distant conurbation. But the terraced houses, their windows ablaze with Christmas trees, clung on to the valley sides. Just like the people who live here. When the mills grew silent and they tore down the weaving sheds and turned them into windy wastelands of willowherb and the kestrels roosted in the cold mill chimneys, when the economic heart of the town gave out, the people hung on. They resisted the lure of a fat wage packet and a suburban dream home. For they'd put down roots in these hills like the mountain ash and the gnarled alder whose bronze catkins tremble under the cold gaze of the stars. And they knew no more why than the trees themselves. Except that it suited them and they drew their own special nourishment from being here.

After the lull of teatime the streets began to grow busy again. Quite a crowd was beginning to form outside the old Co-op grocers, where the ghost of Albert Earnshaw had been seen to wander. His pencil behind his ear he moved around the cool, dark, cavernous interior, easing the fat yellow butter from the butter tubs or winding the handle of the big red bacon slicer. Or weighing out the fruit for the Christmas puddings: currants that shone like birds' eyes, glistening heaps of dates and raisins, mixed peel and sparkling glacé cherries. A ghost conjured from the tribal memory of everyone over fifty, wrapped in the smell of cinnamon and tapers, treacle and boot polish and bathed in the marmalade light of nostalgia.

But today the old Co-op was a video store, and the few benighted souls who wanted to get in there to hire out a hundred and twenty tawdry minutes of blood and guts in technicolour had to fight their way past a pile of trombone and euphonium cases. For this is what had drawn the evening crowd. The local prize band, an assortment of youth and old stagers who had come to tap the rhythm and frost out of their toes on the pavements of the town and play carols. It was an old Christmas custom which had survived the television age by the skin of a bandsman's whiskers. But it was growing more popular again, to wrap up warm as a hamster, round up the children, pop some mince pies in your pocket and a dram in dad's hipflask, and huddle together under the street lamps singing your heart out to 'God Rest Ye Merry Gentlemen'. Perhaps people had taken it up again because they wanted Christmas the way *they* wanted it. Not organised for them by a fat cigar-puffing television executive with an eye on the schedules and a hand in the pocket of the advertisers. Not the mass-produced tinsel of the media, but something to touch their hearts and souls that had its roots in the soil of their own culture.

The haunting notes of the cornet solo at the end of 'When a Child is Born' rose above the warm breath of the crowd, sharpened like icicles and pierced the mute inanimacy of the night. And its beauty pierced the hearts of the silent listeners in the houses around. The Misses Whittaker stopped what they were doing, tilting their heads like watchful hens, their boney, freckled hands resting in their laps. They were doing what they did every Christmas Eve, decorating the crib. It was nothing much. Just an old shoe-box they'd filled with straw begged from the milkman. And dotted around were little animals collected over the years. A squirrel, a hedgehog, two mice, a deer with its antlers chipped off. And a pink baby doll in tiny clothes they'd knitted. A silent, motley tableau placed on the oak sideboard next to the faded family photos and the absent wedding pictures. Sadly pathetic perhaps to an outsider, but to the two sisters a ritual without which Christmas would be incomplete. Their own private, passionate act of homage to the timeless mystery of the Nativity.

Away from the swaddling intimacy of the valley the moors rose dark and hostile. A full moon now shone, bathing the land in a cold, pagan light. Sheep grazed alongside their moon shadows, restless with hunger. They were mean hills, soured by peat bogs, pauperised by the bare outcrops of rock with their wild names. Wolf Stones. Bride Stones. Raven Mire. Wicken Dyke. And the moon was at home in this ancient, heathen landscape, brushing the hills with its pale spores. Clouds that crossed her path rusted like iron water, the very blood of these hills. And the withered hands of the trees that were raised towards her were burnt black for their idolatry. While the winter stars wheeled overhead, lost in the slow solemnity of their magnificent dance.

But a few lights burnt steadily on the moortop, in the farms where men had chosen to take up the unequal struggle against a grudging nature. A winter that lasted seven months of the year and the promise of summer which dissolved in the disappointment of rain and dripping mists. Here, in one of the farms, Reuben Moorhead was doing his final rounds for the night. He swung open the creaking wooden door of the byre and was met by the warm, sweet smell of dung and silage. It was the smell of his life, its essence. He listened to the slow, rhythmical churn as his cattle chewed the cud and felt their heat rising from the stalls. If his animals were content then so was he. His animals were in his blood as they'd been in his father's father's blood and as far back as man and animal had looked upon one another for mutual support. If the truth were known, and it's a sad truth, he loved them more than he loved his fellow man. Soon he would close the door and return to his farmhouse with its cold flagged floor and bare pine table, and he'd be glad to be where he was, away from the town, out there on the frontier, the edge of the wilderness. It held no fears for him, loneliness, isolation. It was the emptiness in men's hearts which frightened him most.

And now it's grown late. A shadowy figure is gliding through the churchyard. It is the vicar come to prepare his church for the midnight service. He enters the porch and the hollow click of the latch and the groan of hinges is the sound of a door being opened on eight hundred years of history. The silent shadows welcomed him as they have done the townspeople down the centuries, men and women whose prayers are part of the stonework, whose hymns of praise still whisper amongst the vaulted arches of the roof. People long forgotten but tangibly linked to the present by the common bonds of faith and sanctified ritual. He switches on the lights and the shadows spring to life, brass and stonework, stained glass and flowers bring a sudden unison of colour and warmth to the ancient darkness.

Down the path in the churchyard other figures are approaching. They stumble and bumble their way towards the porch, for some of them may have had a drink or two. Their thick northern speech falls heavily on the sharp night air. But not unnaturally. For the ancient gravestones around them would have recognised this as the native speech of England unmodified by the niceties of education or the pretentions of class.

'Hey up, Ernest! Tha'll wake the dead.'

But perhaps the dead were already awake? Ranked in celestial halls, ready to carol their hosannas at the anniversary of their king's nativity?

Inside the church they grunt and puff their way up the narrow stone staircase in the tower, the torchlight flickering on their red and jolly faces. The last part of the journey is up a ladder into the bell chamber where the ruffled pigeons glare at them from their perches. Their own giant shadows lope among the dusty rafters. The bitter cold air strikes through the louvres and the men bunch their shoulders and blow their palms. They'll not be cold for long, once they've set to work on the bells. They're here to ring out the midnight Virgin's Chime, a custom old as obscurity. No rope is used, but each man will lie down under a bell, a ton and a quarter above him, and grasping the clapper in both hands will strike it against the bell side.

Far down below the church fills. Old and young, candle-light and excitement alive in their eyes, summoned by magic and mystery, by the story of a birth out of the despair of winter.

The bell tower creaks and shudders into life as the clock stiffens to strike the midnight. The men muffle their ears with their coat collars and scarves. But this will be nothing to the noise they will have to bear when their own bells begin to sound. One, two, three ... The whole town has caught its breath and is counting. The last peal of midnight has barely died away when the bellringers begin. Poised like rowers ready to skim across the vast ocean of the night. Crash go the bells, releasing giant birds of sound which wheel over the moonsoaked rooftops of the town and out onto the moors beyond. Suddenly it seems that from this insignificant, unfashionable and unremarkable town a sound is born that touches everyone who hears it. Something that reaches to the very quick of their humanity. As the earth swings in the coldest reaches of space, as nature hangs limp in the jaws of winter, as mankind in all its variety suffers at the indifferent hand of illness, misfortune and death, it speaks of hope.

The Misses Whittaker hear it as they lie in their lonely beds, the moonlight falling on their home-made crib, and it speaks to them of love and the laughter of children. Reuben Moorhead hears it in his silent, empty farmhouse and it melts the bitterness of his heart. Hilda and Eileen and Her-from-the-Tripe-Stall hear it and it drives out all thoughts of sage-and-onion stuffing and scandal from their minds as they share in the ineffable mystery of the universe. Jack Stansfield hears it, and time, which has stolen so much from him, stands still and unfolds all her riches. Past and present, warm flesh and cold ghosts are united in the embrace of the bells. And as the last chime dies away, the breathless silence of peace and joy settles over the town. It is Christmas Day.